UNDERSTANDING CONTEMPORARY AMERICAN LITERATURE

Matthew J. Bruccoli, Founding Editor

Linda Wagner-Martin, Series Editor

UNDERSTANDING CHANG-RAE LEE

UNDERSTANDING
CHANG-RAE LEE

Amanda M. Page

The University of South Carolina Press

Published by the University of South Carolina Press
Columbia, South Carolina 29208

www.sc.edu/uscpress

Manufactured in the United States of America

26 25 24 23 22 21 20 19 18 17
10 9 8 7 6 5 4 3 2 1

Library of Congress Cataloging-in-Publication Data
can be found at http://catalog.loc.gov/.

ISBN 978-1-61117-782-4 (cloth)
ISBN 978-1-61117-783-1 (ebook)

This book was printed on recycled paper with
30 percent postconsumer waste content.

For Maura and David, the sweetest distractions,
and for Troy, who makes it all possible

CONTENTS

SERIES EDITOR'S PREFACE

The Understanding Contemporary American Literature series was founded by the estimable Matthew J. Bruccoli (1931–2008), who envisioned these volumes as guides or companions for students as well as good nonacademic readers, a legacy that will continue as new volumes are developed to fill in gaps among the nearly one hundred series volumes published to date and to embrace a host of new writers only now making their marks on our literature.

As Professor Bruccoli explained in his preface to the volumes he edited, because much influential contemporary literature makes special demands, "the word understanding in the titles was chosen deliberately. Many willing readers lack an adequate understanding of how contemporary literature works; that is, of what the author is attempting to express and the means by which it is conveyed." Aimed at fostering this understanding of good literature and good writers, the criticism and analysis in the series provide instruction in how to read certain contemporary writers—explicating their material, language, structures, themes, and perspectives—and facilitate a more profitable experience of the works under discussion.

In the twenty-first century Professor Bruccoli's prescience gives us an avenue to publish expert critiques of significant contemporary American writing. The series continues to map the literary landscape and to provide both instruction and enjoyment. Future volumes will seek to introduce new voices alongside canonized favorites, to chronicle the changing literature of our times, and to remain, as Professor Bruccoli conceived, contemporary in the best sense of the word.

Linda Wagner-Martin, Series Editor

ACKNOWLEDGMENTS

I would like to express my sincere appreciation and gratitude to Linda Wagner-Martin for her untiring efforts to mentor a new generation of American literary scholars. A model of dedicated teaching and scholarly generosity, her energy and encouragement have made all the difference.

Thank you to Jennifer Ho at the University of North Carolina at Chapel Hill, who introduced me to many of the texts and concepts that inform this book. Thanks to the English departments at Marywood University and Juniata College for welcoming me to engaging, dynamic, and supportive academic environments while I was at work on this book. Special thanks to Hannah Bellwoar for helping to make the transition from student to professor so much easier. Shout out to my Juniata College Writing Workshop students for their insightful comments on drafts of this book and for pointing out when I need to practice what I teach.

And, finally, much love and gratitude to Troy, Maura, and David Taylor. You are my happiness.

CHAPTER 1

Understanding Chang-rae Lee

With the publication of his debut novel in 1995, Chang-rae Lee became an immediate critical and popular success. For *Native Speaker,* Lee won the American Book Award, the Hemingway Foundation/PEN Award for Best First Novel, and many other honors. His second novel, *A Gesture Life,* was critically lauded when it appeared in 1999. That year the *New Yorker* listed Lee among the twenty best American writers under the age of forty. Lee's subsequent novels, *Aloft* (2004), *The Surrendered* (2010), and *On Such a Full Sea* (2014), have been well-received best sellers like their predecessors. *The Surrendered* won the Dayton Peace Prize and was nominated for the Pulitzer Prize. Now a professor of creative writing at Stanford University, Lee has become a major voice in contemporary American literature.

Chang-rae Lee was born in South Korea on July 29, 1965, to Young Yong and Inja (Hong) Lee. At the age of three he moved to the United States, where his father was completing a psychiatric residency. The family lived briefly in Pittsburgh, Pennsylvania, before moving to the Upper West Side of Manhattan, New York, where Dr. Lee took a position at Bellevue Hospital. The family eventually settled in suburban New Rochelle. In an interview Lee recounted that his primary contact with the Korean community came on Sundays when the family attended a Korean Presbyterian church in Flushing.[1] Lee's biography is different from the usual narratives of first-generation immigrants' struggles with poverty and alienation. Though living in predominately white neighborhoods in Westchester County, Lee did not feel like an outsider and has reported being "fairly well-integrated."[2] He did contemplate changing his name when beginning school but chose to keep Chang-rae.[3] He had a comfortable middle-class suburban childhood, attending boarding school at Phillips Exeter Academy before heading to Yale University to earn a BA in English in 1987.

Lee spent a year working on Wall Street for an investment bank before quitting his job to write his first novel, called "Agnew Belittlehead."[4] Though unpublished, the manuscript helped get Lee accepted into the creative writing program at the University of Oregon. He received his MFA in 1993, the same year he married Michelle Branca, an architect. Lee remained at the University of Oregon until 1998 as an assistant professor of creative writing. After the acclaimed publication of *Native Speaker,* he moved back to the East Coast to create the graduate creative writing program at Hunter College. While at Hunter, Lee taught and befriended the writer Gary Shteyngart; Lee helped him publish his first novel, *The Russian Debutante's Handbook.*[5] With the success of *A Gesture Life* in 1999, Lee joined the creative writing faculty at Princeton University, where he has taught from 2002 until 2016, when he joined Stanford University's faculty. Lee has also repeatedly served as a Shinhan Distinguished Visiting Professor at Yonsei University in Seoul, South Korea. He lives with his wife and two daughters, Eva and Annika.

Despite Lee's personal and professional success, his first novel reflects the outsider tension characteristic of immigrant fiction, which, in turn, influenced the publicity for *Native Speaker* and for the author. The press perpetuated the idea that Lee's novel was the first Korean American–authored book to be published, even though the beginnings of Korean American literature had been established decades earlier with Younghill Kang's novels *The Grass Roof* (1931) and *East Goes West* (1937) and Richard E. Kim's best seller *The Martyred* (1964), among others.[6] *Native Speaker,* however, marked the beginning of a series of popular books by Korean Americans in the second half of the 1990s, as such authors as Susan Choi and Nora Okja Keller published popular and critically acclaimed books.

Because the marketing around *Native Speaker* positioned Lee as the "first" Korean American writer, reviews of his novel often sought to conflate the character of Henry Park with the author. In Pam Belluck's *New York Times* profile of Lee, titled "Being of Two Cultures and Belonging to Neither," she focused on Lee's biography to draw parallels with the novel to suggest Lee's alienation.[7] Also in the *New York Times,* Rand Richards Cooper's review, "Excess Identities," went a step further to suggest that the novel was really "a memoir struggling to get out—a rapturous evocation of a past life, viewed across a great gap of time and culture," and the review concluded that if Lee had "scrapped the spy stuff," it would have been a better read.[8] By presuming the autobiographical significance of the text, the reviewer worked to undermine the book as a work of creative fiction. Cooper went further to suggest that autobiography would be a more appropriate genre for Lee's work. The implication of this suggestion, of course, is that an autobiographical account would be more "authentic" as well as in keeping with the tradition of first-person immigrant literature.[9]

This particular critical response to *Native Speaker* reveals the double-edged nature of being lauded the premier Korean American author. Yoonmee Chang wrote, "Chang-rae Lee, who routinely rejects categorization as an Asian American writer and whose work does not always focus on Asian American characters, finds his success rooted in the reading of his texts as ethnographic autobiography."[10] David Palumbo-Liu has argued that the surge of interest in contemporary Asian American literature requires Asian American authors to follow a narrow set of scripted conventions that seem to suggest answers "to a generalized 'problem' of racial, ethnic, and gendered identities" in order to be successful, answers which then reinscribe what Asian Americans and Asian American literature should be.[11] What is published and accepted by the public, he stated, depends largely on an author's following of predetermined expectations.

The critic Kandice Chuh has noted that "minoritized literatures tend to be coded as '(multi) cultural.' Meanwhile, the 'literary' is reserved for canonical writers and texts. This solution to the multicultural problem creates a divide between 'high' (literary) and 'low' (minority) culture, effectively racializing the idea of culture itself."[12] While seeming to open the doors to creative production from marginalized groups, multiculturalism, according to Chuh, "makes difficult an engagement with minoritized literatures as anything other than ('authentic') artifacts of an ethnography of the Other. Otherness, here, appears principally as an idea, one devoid of contradictions and complexities that inscribe and describe people's lives."[13] The tendency to conflate an author with her/his fictional characters is especially exacerbated if that writer is a member of a minority group.

Reading Lee's novels for the authentic, autobiographical truth of his life—and by proxy for "the Korean American experience"—undermines his position as a fiction writer, an issue that Lee addressed after the publication of his third novel. Reflecting on the reception of *Aloft*'s middle-aged white Italian American narrator, Lee stated: "Indeed the assumption is that before *Aloft* I was writing more from 'experience' rather than employing whatever artistic skill and sensibility I possessed, which is terribly frustrating. All writers work from experience to some extent, of course, and yet there's something about the American reader and culture at the moment that obsesses on the personal, giving primacy to 'reality' narratives and 'essential' identities and ignoring or diminishing the great wonders of imagination."[14] That the racial identities of his protagonists influence how critics read the "truth" of his novels restricts how Lee's work is received. This reception is shaped by his ethnic identity rather than by the work itself—ironic for a work such as *Aloft,* which interrogates white privilege.[15]

Humorously satirizing his own liminal position, Lee in *Aloft* describes the fiction of one of his characters: "he writes about The Problem with Being Sort of Himself—namely, the terribly conflicted and complicated state of being Asian and American and thoughtful and male" (*Aloft* 78). Although he writes with tongue in cheek of this "conflicted and complicated state," Lee must consistently negotiate the labels of "American" and "Asian American" when promoting his work. The difficulty described by Palumbo-Liu of being Asian American in U.S. letters is evident in Lee's need to underscore the American component of his identity: "I'm very comfortable with being an Asian-American writer. That's what I am. What I'm not so comfortable with is how people want to define what Asian-American writers do and what they should say and how they should say it."[16] He has frequently chafed at the limitations that being labeled an "ethnic" writer put on the reception of his work, remarking in one early interview, "People call *Native Speaker* an immigrant novel, but all immigrant novels are American novels at the core": "That novel is a response to what was, I think, becoming expected of Asian American writers, which was that we write these very circumscribed family stories, within-the-house kind of stories, where there's also a keen intergenerational conflict. As wonderful as those stories are, I wanted to widen the stage in which my character was going to act."[17]

Throughout his career Lee has tried "to widen the stage" for how Asian American literature is received as he pushed the thematic and formal boundaries of his work further with each new novel. While his second novel, *A Gesture Life,* is told in the first person by an unreliable Asian American male narrator, just as his debut novel was, Lee moves between the present and the past to merge a contemporary suburban narrative with a historical war story. Lee's third book, *Aloft,* returns to the suburban setting of its predecessor but in a comic vein with an unreliable Italian American narrator who sometimes illustrates a humorous lack of awareness about his own white privilege. This novel was followed by Lee's first book with third-person narration, *The Surrendered,* an ambitious historical epic that covers decades and continents from the perspectives of several characters. His most recent work, *On Such a Full Sea,* is his most daring experiment yet. Set in a dystopian near-future, the novel is told in a strikingly unusual communal voice that tells the mythic tale of a heroine who escapes the narrow life that has been laid out for her. In Lee's work to date, there is a clear desire to move beyond the straightforward domestic novel.

Betsey Huang noted Lee's distaste for reductive biographical questions that suggest his characters are based on real life because of the double standard that allows white authors to "create" while ethnic writers "recount," a distinction that "attests to Lee's privileging of fiction (as a creative endeavor) over autobiography and other forms of life writing."[18] Lee's preference for fiction also serves as a way to avoid having to hold his own life up as the model for Korean American experience. The critic Florian Sedlmeier posited Lee as a "postethnic writer" along with Colson Whitehead, Sherman Alexie, and Jamaica Kincaid, who "defy the protocols of cultural representativeness and seek access to a decidedly literary culture through an investment in literary form and self-reflectivity."[19] Despite the diversity of Lee's canon, each novel shares an investment in paying homage to literary influences. In his work Lee gestures to authors as diverse as Ralph Ellison, Homer, John Cheever, Walt Whitman, and many others. This intertextuality deepens the texture and resonance of each novel while also serving as a reminder that Lee situates his work as serious literary fiction. Lee's insistence on being received first as an artist rather than as a cultural ethnographer or an ethnic memoirist supports critical readings of the texts. As Michelle Rhee argued about *Native Speaker,* "Lee creates his own metafictional rejoinder within his novel by dismantling the stereotype of the model Asian American while subtly addressing the existing challenges for an Asian American writer in multicultural America."[20] He self-consciously engages with the limitations and burdens placed on his work.

While Lee's novels may not be autobiographical, many of his nonfiction essays that have appeared in popular press venues, most frequently in the *New York Times* and the *New Yorker,* were personal accounts. A number of publications were about the loss of his mother to stomach cancer in 1992. In these pieces Lee reflected on her struggle to adapt to life in the United States, her fierce love of her family, and her untimely death at the age of fifty-two. Although all of Lee's novels depict characters with cancer, these memoirs were deeply affecting in the depth and complexity with which Lee confronted the effects of the disease on his mother, his family, and himself.

In a beautiful early essay appearing in the *New England Review* in 1993, Lee told his mother's story in terms of voice, speaking, and language. "The Faintest Echo of Our Language" opens with the scene of her final moments and the silence it brought. Lee introduced the significance of language with his own story of acculturation to the United States. He wrote that he did not speak for his first year of school and that his only friend was a Japanese boy with whom he communicated without words. Despite his mother's painful childhood experience of the Japanese occupation of Korea (a subject Lee indirectly explores in his second novel, *A Gesture Life*), Inja, whose name is a legacy of Japanese colonization, attempted to communicate with his friend's mother in fragments of Japanese and English for her son's sake. Lee soon adapted to American culture and learned English quickly. This facility both pleased and worried his mother: she was happy he was fitting in but concerned that he was losing his ability to speak Korean—the language she was once forbidden to speak as a child.

Unlike his father, who mastered English so well as to "choose a profession where talking is everything," his mother did not become fluent.[21] Lee noted her divided existence as a Korean immigrant: she was confident in her domestic sphere but meek when out in the world. Lee wrote of his resentment at having to be her translator in public, to "do the work of voice" ("The Faintest Echo" 88). He told a story of once refusing to call the bank for her and her inability to fight back; this encounter was recounted again in a later memoir as representative of his teenaged frustrations with her fear: "Suddenly, her life seemed so small to me" ("Coming Home" 167). Yet it was this same "work of voice" that he claimed as an adult at the end of the essay: "I am here to speak. Say the words. Her nearness has delivered me to this moment, an ever-lengthening moment between her breaths, that I might finally speak the words turning inward, for the first time, in my own beginning and lonely language: Do not be afraid. It is all right, so do not be afraid. You are not really alone. You may die, but you will have been heard. Keep speaking—it is real. You have a voice" ("The Faintest Echo" 92). Lee's willingness to speak served as testimony to both his mother's life and her voice. It was also the assertion of Lee's own voice, as the essay spoke their story through his mastery of the language that once divided them.

"The Faintest Echo of Our Language" also showed Lee coming into his own as a writer. Recalling that in high school he wrote stories that were meant to be raceless but were really "some kind of white," he aspired to be "authentic" in the manner of James Joyce, Ernest Hemingway, John Cheever, and Saul Bellow: "I was to breach that various land, become its finest citizen and furiously speak its dialects" ("The Faintest Echo" 90). Such an achievement happened, Lee reported, in this one story in which the protagonist's mother was marked as Asian and in which the son was reunited with his mother and "they do not speak; she simply knows he is home." In claiming his mother—and himself—Lee was able to find his voice and enter the land of literary achievement that he aspired to as a young man.

In another essay Lee used his artist's voice to make a political statement in a brilliantly understated way. "Mute in an English-Only World," published in 1996 in the *New York Times,* was a response to tensions in a New Jersey suburb over signage only in Korean rather than in English. Seemingly sympathetic to those "alienated" by Korean signs in their town, Lee's stories of his mother's struggles with English seem to have explained that surprising sympathy: "I don't doubt that she would have appreciated doing the family shopping on the new Broad Avenue of Palisades Park. But I like to think, too, that she would have understood those who now complain about the Korean-only signs." The essay ends with his wondering if those same people would be sympathetic to her—the answer to which was a subtly implied "no." With the gentle stressing of Lee's own empathy for those excluded by language and creating sympathy for an immigrant's struggle to assimilate, the xenophobic and possibly racist subtext of the "English Only" argument that was so prevalent in the 1990s surfaced. Lee's first novel shares this short article's critique of linguistic domination; both the essay and the novel were Lee's ways of bearing witness to his mother's pain and promoting a more genuinely inclusive America.

In "Coming Home Again," his 1995 memoir in the *New Yorker,* Lee wrote that he had been living in New York City working on his unpublished novel and trying to become a professional writer while his mother was dying of cancer in Syracuse. He returned home to help the family and ended up cooking for his father and his sister, Eunei.[22] With his mother's stomach cancer rendering her unable to eat, Lee threw himself into re-creating her dishes to tempt her appetite. Lee described her *kalbi* recipe in such rich detail that the reader too could make it. Food became a way of expressing love and appreciation, but it also caused physical and psychological discomfort. Food also became a site of conflict for mother and son, as it represented their different experiences of acclimating to American culture. Lee recollected a time when he demanded that his mother learn to make "exotic American dishes" even though his mother struggled to communicate with the neighbor who offered to show her how (a story that Lee recounted again in "Magical Dinners" [2010]) ("Coming Home" 166). He also remembered gorging himself on his mother's Korean cooking to the point of illness when she visited him at Exeter, where the food was bland New England cuisine, the subject of a humorous later memoir called "Immoveable Feast" (2014). The critic Mary Jane Hurst wrote, "The disparate implications here—of food as a crucial element of one's family life, ethnic community, and individual identity but, on the other hand, of gagging, of having to swallow too much, of being overcome by internalizing distinctive elements—indicate the various meanings Lee finds in food."[23]

"Magical Dinners" further dwells on food as a metaphor for assimilation. Although Lee and his sister pined for American food, his parents "want to hold on to what they know" (69). They spent happy Sundays in Chinatown hunting for familiar groceries whose flavors, ultimately, never turned out quite the way they remembered. The essay concludes with a Korean American Thanksgiving, complete with a "buxom and tan" turkey and elaborate Korean side dishes. As

Dr. Lee carved the bird, according to his son, "My mother winces. The knife strobes: the first cut is deep, surprisingly easy" (73). Lee's memories of food revealed his complicated feelings about Korean and American cultures and, in turn, showed his ambivalent feelings toward his mother's unsuccessful acculturation.

In "The Faintest Echo of Our Language," Lee wrote that the "scent from our mother's kitchen protected us and our house, kept at bay the persistent ghosts of the land who seemed to visit everyone else" (86). In "Coming Home Again," he reported that after his mother's death, he and his father "drifted through the rooms like ghosts," so he attempted to cook her food as a comfort but failed to get it right (168). Lee's memoirs reveal a woman with a strong personality and surprising facets (as when her children discovered that she was a basketball star during her Korean girlhood), but his mother's discomfort in the United States had rendered her a ghost of her former self, causing friction between mother and son. Lee wrote, "It puzzled me how much she considered her own history immaterial, and if she never patently diminished herself, she was able to finesse a kind of self-removal by speaking of my father whenever she could" ("Coming Home" 166). In *Native Speaker,* Lee later based a similarly alienated character, called only Ahjuma, on his mother's experiences.[24] In these autobiographical essays, however, Lee used food as a symbol of love: her food nourished and protected the family, and his efforts to cook her food served to show a son's respect and appreciation for his mother's sacrifices.

Lee's food writings run the gamut from humorous to profound, from the poignant story behind his wife's grandmother's recipe for humble fagioli in "Beans" (1996) to his funny love letter to his "monster" gas grill in "My Suburb; Ridgewood, N.J." (2000). In these accounts, food always nourishes more than the body. Several of Lee's travel memoirs blurred the sensual experience of eating with sexual desire, such as his 2002 *New Yorker* essay "Sea Urchin," in which Lee described his first return to Seoul since he had emigrated as a child. His youthful attraction to the girls he saw on his travels became an obsession with sea urchin, a delicacy that both attracted and repulsed him. Food and sex were frequent coconspirators in these essays. A 2000 account of a trip to Thailand with his wife, "The Spicy Pleasures of Phuket," was part history and part travel guide, but its most memorable passages were about a luxury spa treatment that resulted in curried bodies that made the couple hungry. This motif was reminiscent of *Native Speaker,* in which Henry Park's preoccupation with all things oral includes both food and sex.

"Manhattan," a 2012 piece appearing in the *New Yorker,* blurs the boundaries of sensual luxuries, but this time sex and cocktails gave way to Lee's affection for his girlfriend's sophisticated but approachable father. Although this person was of the cultural elite in New York City, Lee found himself better able to talk in depth with this man over manhattans than he was with his father over Genesee cream ales. Lee's essay echoes the reappearing significance of fathers-in-law and surrogate father figures throughout Lee's work. From Henry Park's relationship with Lelia's intimidating father in *Native Speaker* to Paul Pyun's comfortable connection to clueless Jerry Battle in *Aloft*,[25] white fathers-in-law provided examples of white male privilege for Lee's (often) insecure young Asian American male characters. Middle-aged white men provided a window into the confidence that having a secure, unquestioned identity brings—for better or for worse.

If food can denote economic privilege or class aspiration in Lee's work (as when he recounted carefully saving his money at boarding school to buy expensive salami, cheese, and smoked oysters as special treats), it also can serve as a reminder of the value of humility. He valued the terrible homemade wine he was given in Italy and the rustic cuisine he ate in Oregon, the latter meal the result of being "resourceful rather than rich" ("Understanding Oregon Pinot Noir Country" [2009]). In "Immoveable Feast," he nostalgically concluded that the communal dining hall experience at Exeter was character building because "sometimes being catered to is not the most satisfying thing" (64). Food can spur human connection and can become an embodiment of sharing and generosity.

The most consistent element in all of Lee's work, both fiction and nonfiction, is his interest in the depths of human emotion that are hidden beneath the surface of shallow human interactions. It is not surprising, then, to see how the death of Lee's mother corresponded to the birth of his professional writing career, as he discussed in an interview with Bruce Fulton: "I think after my mother died—maybe this happens in all families—it jarred us. It certainly jarred me, and although I was always wanting to write and meaning to write, it jarred me in a different way—it helped my writing. Garret Hong [Lee's mentor at the University of Oregon][26] sometimes says he thinks I was bestowed with her humanity after she died, that just being with her and living through that experience, watching her die, made me more human. Maybe that's true. I think I was never as vulnerable emotionally as I was after she died, and I definitely think that vulnerability is something all writers need if they want to write anything decent."[27] The emotional vulnerability that Lee has attributed to the best writers was the defining characteristic of his personal essays about his mother's death. These early works also demonstrated Lee's command of his narrative voice and the distinctive lyrical style he has brought to his fiction.

In a paragraph-long account of his reaction to the death of J. D. Salinger appearing in the *New Yorker*, Lee told of first reading *The Catcher in the Rye* at age ten and reconnecting to the book later when he was fifteen years old and at boarding school. He recounted being especially taken with Salinger's characters, who are "wounded, exquisitely—with what seemed all the thorny emotion of life and of the world" ("Remembering Salinger" [2010]). This description equally applies to Lee's own works of fiction; all of his novels focus on the complex emotional lives of troubled people: "Like most people, I'm fascinated by characters who are completely flawed personalities, riven by anguish and doubt, and are psychologically suspect. Wait a minute—basically that's everybody, isn't it, in life and on the page? As a writer, I'm drawn to characters who, for one reason or another, seem to find themselves desperately out of joint, alienated but not wanting to be, and ever yearning to understand the rules of the game."[28] Lee's central characters epitomize these characteristics: flawed, out of joint, alienated. His first two novels, *Native Speaker* and *A Gesture Life,* are preoccupied with the benefits and drawbacks of assimilation to culturally alien values and expectations. In *Native Speaker,* Lee's narrator, Henry Park, is a spy who guiltily uses his Asian American insider status to undermine a Korean American political candidate even as he struggles to understand who he is and where he belongs. The sins of the narrator of *A Gesture Life,* however, are in the past, and Doc Hata spends the novel desperately trying to be the model minority representative that his community expects as a means of escaping his memories of his past moral failures. Jerry Battle of *Aloft* is obviously kin to his predecessors in that he, like Henry Park and Doc Hata, is also an "emotional alien" (*Native Speaker* 5).

All of Lee's early narrators are emotionally distant from those around them (particularly the women in their lives) and struggle to connect with the larger world. The emotional dishonesty of these narrators leads to the construction of opaque, unknowable women, whom the reader can reconstruct only through bits and pieces of truth that filter through the untrustworthy narration. Henry's Ahjuma, Hata's K, and Jerry's Daisy remain mysterious and half-formed because the perspectives they are filtered through often deny them subjectivity. The alienation, inner conflict, and self-deception of these unreliable narrators are unifying characteristics and speak to the detachment that Lee's depictions of masculine identity demand—as well as the dangers this emotional withdrawal poses to truly living.

The Surrendered too dwells on emotional disengagement, in this case caused by trauma. Inspired by Lee's father's losses as a boy during the Korean War, the novel follows June Han and Hector Brennan, who are alienated and unable to form lasting relationships. June, the first female character whose consciousness Lee describes, is as emotionally isolated as any of Lee's male characters. She is one of the most intriguing characters of contemporary literature. As is the case with Lee's earlier novels, *The Surrendered* examines how feelings of guilt from complicity in past wrongs work to silence people, divide them from others, and limit their futures. Although all of Lee's characters strive for redemption—or at least a measure of spiritual peace—achieving emotional honesty and true connection to other people is elusive. Subjectivity and citizenship come not from above but from within. Whether taking responsibility for bettering a community or making genuine connections with others on a personal level, the individual self is determined through networks of relationships.

Relationships between parents and children are often the measure of characters' moral redemption. Throughout Lee's novels children—multiracial children in particular—are heavy with symbolic meaning. In his works multiracial children are the potential sites of racial reconciliation, harbingers of a future where racial divisions are irrelevant. Although these children are markers of hope, the burden is great and the relationship between parent and child is fraught with cultural anxiety. In an interview Lee discussed his fears for his (at that time) future children with his wife, Michelle, because they worried that their children would be insecure about their racial identities.[29] Lee's novels are filled with troubled interracial adoptions, miscarried pregnancies, forced abortion, and children's deaths. Three of Lee's five novels to date (*Native Speaker, Aloft,* and *The Surrendered*) include the loss of main characters' children. These characters are meant to represent hope for a better future, but they are doomed, Lee suggests, by the sins of their parents, history, and culture. Ironically, it is in Lee's dystopian novel, *On Such a Full Sea,* dedicated to his daughters, that he imagines a character defined by her transcendence. Like the Virgin Mary, Fan carries a child of hope as told in a myth that sustains a static, emotionally deadened society. Although we know nothing of her inner life, the actions of the enigmatic Fan are the most generous and humane of any taken by Lee's characters. Throughout these novels Lee suggests that only through emotional honesty, cultural reconciliation, and personal engagement can a true life be lived.

CHAPTER 2

"A life univocal"
Native Speaker (1995)

Chang-rae Lee's first novel, *Native Speaker,* remains his most well-known and written-about book. *Native Speaker* was widely acclaimed and won several awards, including the prestigious Hemingway Foundation/PEN Award. The narrator, Henry Park, is a second-generation Korean American who is a spy in his professional life and feels like one in his personal life. The feeling of cultural alienation that torments Henry in his relationships with his Korean-born father and his white American wife are precisely the feelings that serve him well in his job, where he uses his mastery of the rules of assimilation to hide his true self. Although Henry's detachment is a professional asset, his wife, Lelia, sees through his facade and refuses to participate in Henry's performances after the death of their only child, Mitt. At the beginning of the novel, we meet Henry as he works to reevaluate his marriage, work, and identity in the wake of losing his family.

As discussed in chapter 1, the critical treatment of Park as a fictional extension of the author is one variation on a larger assumption by readers: that Park should be a representative of the Korean American experience and that Lee is obligated to engage in respectability politics through his writing. The critic Min Hyoung Song noted that while critics and the author might wish to universalize the reception of the novel, the book's popularity becomes "de facto commentary on Korean American life for many readers."[1] Some readers, in fact, concluded that this representation of an unreadable Asian American spy was stereotypical and damaging.[2] However, the dearth of experience with Korean American literature on the part of readers puts undue pressure on Lee to accommodate that ignorance. This burden overdetermines what Asian American literature must do, as Patricia Chu wrote: "One of the central ideological tasks accomplished by Asian American literary texts is the construction of Asian American subjects through the transformation of existing narratives about American identity. To accomplish these fundamental tasks, Asian American writers have had to address the dislocations particular to Asian immigration, the average American's unawareness of Asian American history and culture, and the deeply entrenched presumption that Asian Americans are not American."[3]

Lee, as have marginalized writers before him, presents his work in a literary context that demands his work prove its legitimacy as "Asian American" before being considered as simply literature. As David Cowart wrote, "Chang-rae Lee must also rise above restrictive expectations predicated on the narrow demands of identity politics. In the event, he fashions a work that, never reductive, eschews any and all such easing posturing, especially the tonalities of 'stridency' and 'righteousness.'"[4] Sunny Xiang suggested that literary critics, like popular readers looking for pat ethnic identification, have embraced the novel because of its blending of literary artistry with "the political recuperation of voice" in a manner that best serves the overall political project of Asian American scholarly criticism.[5]

Liam Corley has seen Lee directly engaging with the limitations of being an "ethnic" writer: "The book's title draws attention to Lee's self-conscious complicity in the racial marketing of his book, and the ambiguity surrounding the novel's 'native speaker' . . . sharpens the edge of the novel's paratextual critique."[6] Even though the book benefited from the marketing that promoted it as exotic "ethnic" fiction, the content of the book pushes back against the confines that this label implies to critics and general readers alike, and it reinforces what Jonathan Arac has seen as Lee's greatest similarity to Ralph Ellison: "career-long vigilance concerning the limits of sociology for minority representation, and the need for literature if the realities of humans living are to be grasped."[7]

Far from shying away from racial stereotypes, the novel begins with a list of labels. Upon leaving him, Henry's wife leaves behind a list of his characteristics that Henry first mistakes for a "love poem." In the list Lelia calls him, among other unflattering things, a "B+ student of life," an "illegal alien," an "emotional alien," and "yellow peril: neo-American" before concluding with "stranger/follower/traitor/spy" (*Native Speaker* 5). Lee directly plays with common accusations applied to Asians in America,[8] with Henry introducing these words as "visions of me in the whitest raw light, instant snapshots of the difficult truths native to our time together" (1). By defining Henry in these particular racist terms, she is also defining her whiteness. But Henry does not reject Lelia's list. Instead he makes multiple copies of it and destroys the original, a signal to the reader that the "real" Henry is only partially represented by the multiple versions of himself that we encounter throughout the novel.

"False speaker of the language" is another entry that Henry finds on a scrap of paper (6). This accusation he accepts as true; he admits to misrepresenting the nature of his work as a spy. Tina Chen argued, "As Henry discerns the paradoxical truth that the masks he wears prevent him from speaking even as they are the very things that enable him to articulate a semblance of self, readers of *Native Speaker* discover that Lee's novel itself operates behind the mask of the spy story in order to expose the formal limitations of narration in Henry's story but also to acknowledge the important role conventions play in dictating the stories by which we know ourselves and others."[9] Henry concludes that "the truth, finally, is who can tell it," reminding us to be critical of all that Henry does say but also to reflect on what he does not say (7). The truth of the story relies on the truth of Henry's identity, something that may be beyond his control. In this first chapter we see that Henry is adept in his use of language and that this skill that serves him well in his career is what makes him untrustworthy in his marriage and as a narrator of his own life.

The phrase "false speaker of the language" resonates deeply with Henry because his unstable sense of self is best illustrated through his complicated relationship with language. Although Korean was spoken in his home, Henry is most adept in English—a fluency that he struggled to achieve through humiliating English-as-a-second-language (ESL) classes that emphasized his racial and cultural difference from his American peers. Crystal Parikh wrote, "Throughout the novel . . . Lee conceives of the execution of language as literally a bodily act. It is an act that is meant to be seamless performance of the continuities of body, identity, and culture, but it often instead exposes the construction of these connections through the processes of education and cultural negotiation."[10] Because Henry's language does not cohere to the expected associations with his racialized body in the context of U.S. society, we see him alter his performances in reaction to those around him who are more secure in their identity constructions. His double consciousness is best illustrated in his relationships with his father and his wife, both of whom he has studied carefully in order to perform his roles. His Asian father embodies the Korean language with which Henry is no long fluent. His white wife embodies American English, the language he has worked to master.[11] His relationships with these characters, like his relationship to language, are strained by Henry's inability to reconcile his bilingual self.

While Henry uses his language to downplay his Korean identity, Lelia claims to recognize his difference at their first meeting by noting that it is not his face but his carefulness when speaking that gives away that he is "not a native speaker" (12). She is drawn to his hidden self, even as she laments her own status as "an average white girl [with] no mystery anymore. . . . Literally nothing to her name." For Henry, a man with two names, it is Lelia's privileged position as "average," as the default, that in turn intrigues him. As he studies her, he stresses both her physical whiteness and her mastery of the language: "What I found was this: that she could really speak. At first I took her as being exceedingly proper, but I soon realized that she was simply executing the language. She went word by word. Every letter had a border" (10).

Lelia's use of language shows her confidence in her identity; Henry's description of it suggests clear delineation of what is "proper" and what is not. It is Lelia's privilege that makes her the arbiter of his linguistic performance. To gain her acceptance, he sizes her up and does "all that blind math so that I might cast for her the perfect picture of a face" (13). His hyperawareness of her privilege—and his own sense of inferiority—drives him to calculate an identity that will win her over.[12] Henry is attracted to her privilege, noting that her father, the type of man whose "trim old body said it all over in simple, clear language: Chief Executive Officer," is part of the reason he loves her: "what it was about Lelia that I desired and feared came partly through his bloodline running through her, the openness and exuberance and all that hard focus she could sometimes call up" (119). To Henry, his father-in-law's white body speaks, and it is his whiteness—and his daughter's—that allows for this type of personality that attracts and frightens Henry. Winning Lelia works to stake a claim to that identity and that privilege.

As the self-acknowledged "standard bearer," Lelia has a linguistic authority that suits her profession as a speech therapist. Henry's experience with speech therapy as a child was painful. Beaten by an "ancient chalk-white woman" whenever he stumbled over a recitation of challenging lines from Percy Bysshe Shelley's *Prometheus Unbound,* Henry's first experience with learning English was torturous.[13] Though his moments of misspeaking as an adult are overlooked, Henry feels the discrepancy as showing his fractured identity: "I always hear myself displacing the two languages, conflating them—maybe conflagrating them—for there's so much rubbing and friction, a fire always threatens to blow up between tongues. Friction, affliction" (234). The friction of Henry's languages is also the friction of his marriage. By marrying Lelia, he is also claiming a mastery of English and his successful assimilation to American culture even as his sense of inferiority remains.[14] In addition, though Lelia's methods of teaching English as a second language are far gentler than those Henry experienced as a child, the fact of her status as a teacher of the language ties her to the "supremacy" that his white teachers and classmates enforced in their policing of the English language.

Henry's father, who took (but did not use) the name George Washington Park upon arriving in the United States, worked his way to wealth by running a greengrocery that he started from capital gained by membership in a Korean money club called a *ggeh*. Though his success was due in part to support from the Korean American immigrant community, he wanted his family to assimilate to American culture, as his choice of adopted name suggests.[15] An adult Henry has noted that as his father moved into the middle class, the less connected to other Koreans he became as his new wealth permitted him to move into the upscale, largely white suburbs outside the city, effectively isolating the family from other immigrants (273).[16]

Despite his economic success, Henry's father has a strained relationship with his son, and language becomes their primary battleground. Henry learns from his father how to use English as a weapon. When fighting with Henry's mother, who was fluent only in Korean, his father would switch into English "as though he had suddenly introduced a switchblade into a clean fistfight" (63). Henry would then use his greater mastery of English to humiliate his father against his mother's wishes, emphasizing the limits of his father's ability to assimilate fully. His father remains proud of his son's mastery despite the difference it has created between them. When his father wants him to speak "some Shakespeare words" in front of their customers to demonstrate the family's assimilation, Henry instead insists on using his "best Korean" when speaking to the other workers so that he remains invisible in the shop to other Americans (53). Henry, who has become so unused to hearing his Korean given name, Byong-ho, that he is startled when he hears it, is motivated by anger and alienation rather than solidarity with other Korean workers.[17]

Henry's refusal to use language in the way that his father wishes is his emotional reaction to his father's frequent absence of language. Silence, as much as speech, is emotionally fraught in Henry's childhood home. He tells Lelia that his mother was "good" but that she "treated it [motherhood] like a job. She wasn't what you'd call friendly. Never warm" (221). This formal parenting style led his parents to conceal from him the extent of his mother's illness from liver cancer; they intentionally misrepresented what was happening. When telling of his father's conspicuous silence after the death of his mother when he was only ten years old, Henry recounts that he never heard his father speak of love "in any language" (58). His father does make an effort to be present for Henry, but it is a silent, uncommunicative presence that does not reveal his grief to his son. Upon Henry's father's death, Lelia writes a poem about cleaning out his house and finding his belongings impersonal; she then wonders if this lack of intimacy continues on in his son.[18] While his Korean remains limited, Henry has learned how to use language and silence to hide himself from others.

The lack of intimacy that so worries Lelia is most egregious when she discovers that Henry does not know the name of the Korean housekeeper who ran his household after his mother's death. An immigrant with little English, the woman called only "Ahjuma" had been brought to America only months after Henry's mother's death essentially to replace the domestic labor his mother had been doing in their home. One day Henry had returned home to find this stranger cooking his mother's recipes and wearing her apron (77).[19] Ahjuma had no friends, family, or interests, and Henry had discovered her sexual relationship with his father as a college student. Lelia cannot believe that Henry knows so little of this woman who, in her view, "practically raised" him (69). The critics You-me Park and Gayle Wald wrote, "She is never properly named in the text but remains throughout 'Ah-ju-ma,' a Korean name for a woman of no significance (similar to 'Auntie' in the U.S.), and is never interpellated by the outside world. Whether it is true that she 'preferred it that way' remains unclarified and unclarifiable because the reader never gets a glimpse into her consciousness. Denied interiority, 'Ah-ju-ma' occupies a curious (but predictable in representations of domestic workers) mode of hyperprivatized existence in which she has no access to individualized subjectivity."[20] Although she appears only briefly in the novel, Ahjuma's vacant presence is symbolically significant to the novel. In counterpoint to *Native Speaker*'s preoccupation with "the legitimation of a male immigrant subject in the public sphere," Korean women "are denied any meaningful access to the public sphere."[21] In addition, while the novel feminizes this denial, the cypher of Ahjuma highlights the majority of immigrant laborers with no voice in this country. Refused individuality, this character cannot participate in public life. Henry fears that he too will be made invisible for his connection to this outsider woman and all those silent immigrants she represents.

Henry's memories of Ahjuma naturally evoke parallel memories of his mother: she, like Ahjuma, was never comfortable with English or America.[22] We learn only through subtext that his mother was depressed as well as ill, staying in her room in her pajamas for long periods of time because "the climate was never quite suitable for her" (135). Henry realizes that, as with Ahjuma, his father never used his mother's name, so that Henry must think to remember it. As with his wife's death, Henry's father "suffered in his own unspeakable and shadowy way" when Ahjuma died unexpectedly (81).

Because of these early relationships, Henry is suspicious of language's ability to express emotion. He reflects that he "never felt comfortable" with saying "I love you" (112). This confession is especially meaningful as Henry thinks of his son, Mitt. Though Henry is uncomfortable expressing love through language, he notes that Lelia spoke to their son with "much care . . . so unstudied, calm. I thought how lucky he was to have had a woman like her directing his life" (112). Neither his father's silence nor his mother's anxiety has provided Henry with a similarly easy, confident ability to express love. His American son, however, had mastery of his language: "Mitt always spoke beautifully, if I remember anything. Lelia read to him every night since he was a year old. She wanted me to read him stories, too, but I never felt comfortable reading aloud, even when I was in high school and college, and I didn't want to fumble or clutter any words for the boy just as he was coming to the language. I feared I might handicap him, stunt the speech blooming in his brain, and that Lelia would provide the best example of how to speak. My silliness. I should have watched and listened" (239). The tragedy of Mitt's death forces Henry to reflect on how his own fears and sense of inferiority limited his relationship with his son.

Henry's deference to Lelia's "best example" is one of many instances when Henry demonstrates his internalized white supremacy. David Cowart has argued that Mitt, whose name he reads as "Mutt," is "another site or body for the drama of assimilation," as when Henry accuses Lelia of regretting Mitt's racial appearance at birth only to recognize "this shameful, half-conscious wish as his own."[23] Henry recognizes his own "assimilist sentiment" as wrong, but his wish for his son is that Mitt will "grow up with a singular sense of his world, a life univocal, which might have offered him the authority and confidence that his broad half-yellow face could not" (267). Speaking Korean and English have been detrimental to developing a coherent identity in Henry's own experience, so his wish for Mitt is to protect him from similar pain without considering the value of a polyvocal life.

Despite Henry's fears, however, young Mitt proves himself able to navigate his biracial identity with more confidence than his father does his bicultural one: "When Mitt played with my father their communication was somehow wholly untroubled, perfect in its way, and if there were questions between them the boy would simply repeat what the old man said, try to echo his pidgin, his story, learn that talk, too. I suppose they could build a bridge because they needed one. I was too close to the old man, we were always within striking distance of each other. We were intently inarticulate, competitively so. But I thought that Mitt was beginning to appreciate the differences in the three of us; he could mimic the finest gradations in our English and Korean, those notes of who we were, and perhaps he could imagine, if ever briefly, that this was our truest world, rich with disparate melodies" (239–40). Born in the United States, Mitt has none of his father's anxiety about language and none of the generational strain that marks his grandfather's relationship with his father. His ability to "appreciate the differences" suggests to Henry the possibility of a better world through the figure of his son. As the grandson of a naturalized

Korean American and an American veteran of the Korean War, Mitt represents reconciliation and unification. Henry sees Mitt's body as "beautifully jumbled and subversive and historic" (103). To Henry, multiracial, multilingual, multicultural Mitt is the embodied hope for a new, more inclusive conception of an American.

This inclusion is tested when Mitt is bullied and called racial slurs by the white boys living in his grandfather's Westchester neighborhood. Henry notes that while Mitt learned to "trash-talk" that summer, "there isn't anything good to say to an average white boy to make him feel small . . . there's a shield in the language, there's no fair way for us to fight" (243–44). He tells Lelia his own theory about the disputed origins of the slur "gook": the American slur for Koreans is in fact the word "America," *Mee-gook* in Korean (242). As in the bastardization of *Mee-gook,* Mitt's racist encounter works to reinforce his American identity; it is his very confrontation with racism that defines him as American. Mitt's confrontation with racism triggers Henry's childhood memories of racist bullying. He recalls his father's respectful and self-effacing approach to speaking to other parents when Henry was a bullied child; this is in sharp contrast to his explosive reaction when doing the same for his grandson. Embarrassed and wanting to silence his father, Henry nonetheless lets him yell in defense of his grandson. This protective impulse is meant for Mitt but resonates with Henry as a corrective to the past.

Mitt bridges the difference between him and the white neighborhood boys, becoming friends with them despite his racist reception. But these hard-won friendships directly lead to Mitt's death when the boys crush him in a playful "dog pile" at his birthday party. Mitt is killed by an "adoring [lynch] mob" of "pale little boys," smothered by whiteness until he too is "pale" in death: "You can hear the attempt of his breath, that unlost voice, calling us from the bottom of the world" (106–7). Mitt's seeming success in assimilating to Westchester is his undoing. Though this symbol of hope is literally crushed, Lou Freitas Caton has seen Mitt as Christ-like in his death: too good for this earth, he is sacrificed for the sins of the world.[24] Sami Ludwig too has argued that Mitt is a figure of redemption and that his "legacy survives as speech."[25] David Cowart viewed Mitt's death more pessimistically: "it implies that hybridity carries its own doom like a virus."[26]

Mitt's death exacerbates the communication problems in Henry's marriage as Lelia finds his silence after their loss impossible to breach. After she leaves him, Henry throws himself into his work for Glimmer and Company, an agency that specializes not in impersonal corporate espionage, as his wife believes, but in spying on individuals. His boss, Dennis Hoagland, sets up his firm to provide "ethnic coverage" (18): "Each of us engaged our own kind, more or less. Foreign workers, immigrants, first-generationals, neo-Americans" (17). Henry uses his insider status as an Asian American to ingratiate himself in the lives of unsuspecting people, and then he writes detailed reports for his client. Henry's gift for language—and his emotional detachment from those around him—makes him a talented spy. He describes his task as an act of "transcription"; he is to be a "clean writer" whose job is to "simply know character. Identity. This is the all" (203). His job is simply to use his ability to blend into a scenario and observe without judgment or even engagement since he is not the one who takes action on his intelligence. He is so good at his job that Hoagland uses Henry's reports as the models for other spies to live up to.

But Henry's insecurity in his own identity and place in the world is also an asset to Hoagland. Jodi Kim has linked Henry's gift for spying to his status as part of the "model minority":

> Here is the model minority myth taken to its logical, linguistic end. In many ways, Henry accepts Lelia's charge that he is a false speaker of language. He is creative only insofar as he is able to mimic the language granted to him by Hoagland, but Henry cannot articulate a language that can reconstitute social relations differently. That his perfect English teaches others how to do the job well arises from his ability to speak the language of power with the same kind of exactitude as that with which he views the city in its spatial relations. Language, like space, is functional, in the service of those who occupy the apex of the racial triangle; Henry's job, which he performs brilliantly as a model minority spy, is to ensure the triangle's maintenance, to weed out potential insurgencies that may threaten the racial order.[27]

Henry understands how the racial order works, but his position as an Asian American places him outside the binary white-black dynamic that dominates U.S. racial discourse. As the "model minority," Henry privileges whiteness, which makes him valuable to Glimmer and Company. Hoagland jokes that white Americans "generally made the worst spies" because they are too flamboyantly sure of themselves (172). Tina Chen wrote, "Henry's efforts to remove himself from his narratives emblematize as well as perpetuate his lack of agency as an Asian-American spy. In order to find voice and expression, Henry must move away from his position as 'a clean writer' and acknowledge his own investments in the stories he writes."[28] Henry's insecurity and alienation—qualities that drive him to master English, to be better than the average native speaker—are what make him so well suited to his career. These are also what cause his detachment in his personal life.

Crystal Parikh has expressed the belief that Lee's choice to depict Henry as a spy "allegorizes the crisis of the 'ethnic intellectual'" by showing a man who betrays his "own" by revealing too much of the group's dirty laundry to outsiders, a danger that Lee risks in writing a book that can be misread as ethnography.[29] Michelle Rhee too sees Lee engaging with the minefields of minority representation: "Creating a strategy of metafiction that inflects the language of the novel, Lee responds to threats against and between Asian Americans through quiet confrontations and manages to critique certain motives in literary gatekeeping practices."[30] This, Rhee argues, shows Lee rejecting the political expectations for his works from both within and without Asian American critique.

Tina Chen has argued that, unlike the genre convention of the savvy (white male) spy with agency, "Lee deliberately reworks the genre of the spy story, altering it to accommodate the exigencies of a spy whose racially determined invisibility signals not license but a debilitating erasure of self and power."[31] J. Paul Narkunas too has read Henry's work at Glimmer and Company as undermining the concept of agency, with Lee presenting "an alternative form of conceiving humans not as subjects, national or otherwise, but as relations of force or figurations that do not add up to a coherent substance."[32] Glimmer and Company views identity as a product that can be sold (329), and Henry merely gathers material to be turned over to higher ups without knowing the endgame, which reveals the larger network of power and position that really determines a person's fate.

Throughout the novel Lee also uses the language of metanarrative to highlight this sense of the expected conventions of genre determining one's fate. It is storytelling that leads to Henry's professional undoing. Assigned to gather intelligence on Dr. Emile Luzan, a Filipino psychiatrist who secretly raises funds to support Marcos back in the Philippines, Henry takes on a "legend"—a fictitious autobiography—and becomes his patient. But the death of Mitt and the separation from Lelia weaken Henry's focus, and he finds himself mixing the truth of his life into his story to receive "comfort" from Luzan (22). Luzan directs Henry to "take up story-forms," and this leads to the breakdown of Henry's "clean" writing style: "His method with me was in fact anti-associative, and he asked me to look at my life not just from a singular mode but through the crucible of a larger narrative. He said he could learn much about me from the way I saw myself working in the world. Is this what I have left of the doctor? That I no longer can simply flash a light inside a character, paint a figure . . . with a momentary language, but that I know the greater truths reside in our necessary fictions spanning human event and time?" (206). Henry's very "mode" of existence is shaken by his sessions with the doctor. Throughout *Native Speaker,* Lee presents Henry using a different "mode" for each new context; his chameleonlike behavior shifts for each new audience as he sizes up a mark's "singular" story. By expanding his perspective to see depths in other people's stories, and his own, Henry gains enough empathy to question the value of his character sketches—easy markers of identity that do not touch the depth of a person's true story—and question his role in producing them, much as Lee resists relying on easy identification to tell his story.

In the larger narrative of the novel, readers must read as the analyst does in order to judge Henry, our unreliable narrator. Although Hoagland reminds Henry that "to be a true spy of identity . . . you must be a spy of the culture" (204), it is culture that draws Henry to Luzan. The informality of their doctor-patient relationship starts with the recognition of psychoanalysis being a Western construct, so that the normal rules do not apply to them (43). Luzan situates much of Henry's pain in the context of being Asian American[33] (133). This feeling of solidarity and understanding along with Henry's desire to connect with another Asian father figure make him forget the rules of his business: he loses control of his story to the point that Luzan prescribes medication (181), and through the subtext of what he says during analysis, Henry even indirectly warns Luzan of the danger he is in (206). Chen noted that Henry's "multiple betrayals" lead to the "unraveling of both his narrative and [his] identity."[34] Hoagland realizes that Henry is a liability and pulls him from his assignment; in Henry's case, the cultural identification makes him vulnerable rather than powerful.

After Luzan drowns in the Caribbean in mysterious circumstances, Hoagland merely reminds Henry, "We do what we're paid for and then who can tell what it means?" (45). But Henry struggles to return to his previous way of being. Parikh wrote that Henry's guilt over Luzan "deviates from the emotional neutrality and distance that the spy must maintain," so as Henry's morality is awakened, he loses his standing in the firm.[35] His loss of control bleeds over into his next assignment, spying on the Korean American city councilman John Kwang, who, Henry notes, would have been close to his father's age (23). Henry is drawn to Kwang on a deeply personal level, identifying with him as a fellow Korean immigrant even more strongly than he did with the Filipino Luzan. Tasked with writing up Kwang's character for Glimmer and Company, Henry recognizes that there are many versions to tell and that Hoagland is not interested in the story of Kwang's loss of family in the Korean War, his extreme poverty as an immigrant, his eventual mastery of English, or his identity as an American: "And where he began to think of America as a part of him, maybe even his, and this for me was the crucial leap of his character, deep flaw or not, the leap of his identity no one in our work would find valuable but me" (211). Kwang's ability to claim American identity for himself is something that Henry finds compelling and out of reach. Lori Jirousek noted, "Losing the cool detachment of the spy, Henry starts to immerse himself more as ethnographer and become deeply involved with what and whom he observes. He finds himself interested in Kwang, not to betray him as a spy, but to understand him anthropologically: to uncover how one becomes a contemporary, successful immigrant."[36]

John Kwang becomes more than a model for a new type of assimilation, however; Henry serves as Kwang's double throughout the novel. As Henry literally plays the role of Kwang's stand-in while staging his political appearances, the line between Henry and Kwang is blurred in Henry's telling of his story, so much so that Henry is even mistaken for Kwang on occasion despite their physical differences. Henry's identification with Kwang prevents him from writing in his usual frank manner the report that Hoagland assigned. Instead he sends pages and pages of useless writing. Henry notes, "My recollection and sight are focused elsewhere now. I am seeing a different story. As I flesh out the day's register, as I am tonight, I feel as if I am desperately prospecting for an alibi, one mine more than Kwang's. The teller, I know, can keep his face in the shadows only so long" (204). The detached Henry could write a person's life as a simple, straightforward narrative and feel no guilt for propagating this singular vision. Luzan's advice to alter his method of storytelling opens Henry up to a wider world with a multiplicity of truth.

This need for an "alibi" also indicates Henry's complicity and guilt as a cultural spy. John Kwang's role as an Asian American politician trying to break down racial divisions in his community is presented in the language of family but without the emphasis on biology or blood. Henry marvels that Kwang makes people of all races feel as though he is giving himself to them as a "brother" (138), when Henry did not think a Korean man could be "a larger public figure who was willing to speak outside of the tight sphere of his family" (139). Unlike Henry, who was raised to look out only for the well-being of his biological family, Kwang "loved the pure idea of family as well, which in its most elemental version must have nothing to do with blood" (146). Part of Kwang's appeal to Henry is in his attempts to move beyond the collectivity of the small family unit or even the solidarity of ethnic or cultural affiliation.

In *Impossible Subjects: Illegal Immigrants and the Making of America*, Mae M. Ngai traced the trajectory of immigration law in the United States during the twentieth century to show how immigration law shaped—and continues to shape—the racial and ethnic makeup of the country. At the turn of the twentieth century, Congress, motivated by racist fears of "yellow peril," passed laws meant to bar Asians from immigrating to the United States. Although the McCarran-Walter Act of 1952 "ended Japanese and Korean exclusion" and "established a new set of norms of desirability based on educational level, skill, and familial ties to Americans,"[37] not until passage of the Immigration Act of 1965 did the United States stop using race to determine eligibility for immigration: "Thus the immigration of Asians and the Asian American population grew phenomenally in the last decades of the twentieth century. . . . The population of Asian Americans grew from less than 1.2 million in 1965 to some 10.0 million in 2000."[38] Asian Americans were not the only beneficiaries of the new immigration law; the overall racial makeup of immigrants to the United States changed rapidly with the end of national origins quotas.[39]

To reach these new, diverse populations, Kwang presents a political vision of a collectivity that transcends identity politics by embracing a multiplicitous American identity. Henry reflects on Kwang's political method: "But can you really make a family of thousands? One that will last? I know he never sought to be an ethnic politician. He didn't want them to vote for him solely because he was colored or Asian. He knew he'd never win anything that way. There aren't enough of our own. So you make them into a part of you. You remember every one of their names. You are the model by which they will work and live. You are their hope. And all this because you are such a natural American, first thing and last, if something other in between" (326). Kwang embraces the differences among people even as he becomes the means of collective unification. The mix of individuality (the cult of Kwang's personality) and collectivity (the unifying interests of immigrants) becomes a more inclusive vision for American identity. Kwang's desire to transcend the "ethnic" label is both pragmatic and idealistic. The hope he offers his constituents is the promise of a better America that lives up to her ideals.[40]

As Betsey Huang noted, Kwang's ability to speak in the public sphere "immediately strikes the reader as a different kind of Asian American, as well as a different kind of *American*."[41] Far from internalizing the invisibility that Henry feels as an Asian American, Kwang has a success that lies in his bold visibility and active participation in his adopted country. Huang further argued that "Kwang's outspokenness and eloquence, the defining factors of his political success, reflect Lee's recognition of the importance of speech and the assertion of voice as the most fundamental means by which citizens and subjects claim and express their membership in American society."[42] Speech—and the confident belief in his right to a voice in American culture—is what separates Kwang's experience and Henry's. But Kwang's voice is impeded by the limited American vocabulary of race: "Soon there will be more brown and yellow than black and white. And yet the politics, especially minority politics, remain cast in terms that barely acknowledge us. It's an old syntax" (196). While Kwang tries to find a new vocabulary for understanding solidarity, he nonetheless must work within a system that renders Asian Americans and Latina/os invisible.

Kwang feels solidarity with African Americans and other marginalized groups in the city; he witnessed segregation in the American South and admired the black power movement in New York City. But because he is Korean American, Kwang must navigate a landscape in which there is assumed racial bias for every position he takes. He tries to bridge racial barriers to connect with the black community but feels like a suspicious "token" at NAACP meetings (194). Noting that excitement around his political career most often happens after an episode of racial unrest, Kwang asks Henry, "How do you say no to what seems like a compliment?" Though he is ostensibly talking about his political reception, his question resonates with the dilemma caused by the American mythos of the Asian American "model minority." Park and Wald observed that the model minority construct demands that Asian American problems be hidden from public view, while African American troubles are publically discussed and held up for ridicule; this dichotomy serves to uphold Asian Americans as examples of self-sufficiency against African American dependence, but it ultimately is in service to white power.[43] How do you overcome a "privileged" social position when you know it is predicated on the very racism that encumbers you? Kwang imagines a Korean American politician who can overcome the triangulation of races[44] that impedes interracial solidarity.[45]

However, the idealism that Kwang's character represents is tested by systems of white supremacy that a single individual cannot subvert. In the midst of Kwang's term, tensions come to a head between the black community and Korean grocers in the city. Writing in 1995, Lee clearly adapted the events of the 1992 Los Angeles uprising after the acquittal in the police brutality case after the Rodney King beating. In "Towards Interracial Understanding and Identification," Kun Jong Lee argued that Chang-rae Lee fictionalizes key historical details to shape his message: the real teenaged Latasha Harlins becomes a black mother shot in the back and killed by an anonymous Korean business owner; and Edward Lee, killed by "friendly fire" while protecting Korean American–owned property as part of a community call to action, becomes a Korean American student who dies in his family's store after it is firebombed.[46] The first change, the critic suggested, deflates stereotypes about criminal black teens and model Asian Americans, while the second change "shows a sanitized version of the Los Angeles riots" that removes the significance of "interracial violence on the collective level."[47] Lee's alterations serve to show the Korean American perspective missing from most media coverage of the time while simultaneously refusing to endorse African American stereotypes.

Native Speaker in many ways serves to counter mainstream interpretations of racial dynamics in Los Angeles. The political scientist Claire Jean Kim has argued that the familiar narrative of conflict between blacks and Koreans is largely a myth that began in the 1970s and conveniently sidesteps the role of white supremacy in creating and maintaining that story. While Kim acknowledges some truth to the argument that "historical discrimination, economic competition, Black rage, immigrant dreams and prosperity" caused conflict, the "racial scapegoating story" misses the bigger truth: "The problem is that the racial scapegoating story isolates these features and rips them out of the overall context of how *racial* power operates in contemporary America."[48] Lee's novel, while dwelling at length on African American–Korean American conflict, also carefully reveals who benefits from this division through John Kwang's experience of politics as a Korean American. Even though his own district is untroubled, Kwang is asked to speak as the Korean spokesman, but "his sympathy for either side was a bias for one" and limits what he is able to say or do in response (193). The white mayor, suggestively named De Roos,[49] is able to sidestep scrutiny and lay blame on his black police commissioner. The mayor in fact benefits from the unrest because "it's a race war everyone can live with" (181). David Palumbo-Liu has written of the way that the racial dynamics of the L.A. "riots" worked to maintain white supremacy:

> In 1992, a little over a quarter of a century after Watts, in another "race riot" in the same city, Korean Americans were represented as the frontline forces of the white bourgeoisie. Not only were they successful even under the most oppressive circumstances, they were not afraid to arm themselves against blacks and Latinos to protect what is not only their territory, but also the buffer zone between the core of a multiethnic ghetto and white middle-class America. The locating, real and figurative, of Asians in *between* the dominant and minor is made less tenuous and even rationalized by a particular element that situates Asians within the dominant ideology and frees them of the burden of their ethnicity and race while retaining (for obvious ideological purposes) the signifier of racial difference: the notion of *self*-affirmative action informs the core model minority myth.[50]

This "race war" takes attention away from structural racism in the city, thus preventing any real change from taking place. Kwang must work to defuse the tensions before he can accomplish any of his political goals.

Lee repeatedly illustrates how racial triangulation works throughout the narrative. Henry recalls his father's battles with a black customer: "They fight like lovers, scarred, knowing. Their song circular and vicious. For she always comes back the next day, and so does he. It's like they are here to torture each other. He can't afford a store anywhere else but where she lives, and she has no other place to buy a good apple or fresh loaf of bread" (186). Caught in the same net, neither can escape the larger structures that force them into conflict. Kwang too acknowledges the racist forces at work by explaining to his constituents in a rousing speech how structural racism keeps African Americans from opening their own businesses in their own neighborhoods (153). He further tries to build affinity across the divided communities by conflating the history of African American slavery with the Japanese colonial occupation of Korea by using the language of enslavement for both experiences.[51] Kwang concludes his speech with a call to unity: "Know that what we have in common, the sadness and pain and injustice, will always be stronger than our differences" (153). In this work written before the Obama presidency, Lee imagines a politician who actively tries to confront racist historical legacies as a way of moving forward together, a project that resonates with contemporary theories of Asian American identity. Lisa Lowe, for example, has argued for a broader understanding of citizenship and solidarity when considered in the context of Asian immigration: "The specific history of Asian immigration in relation to U.S. citizenship is different from the histories of other migrant or racialized groups, such as African Americans, Native Americans, and Chicanos/Latinos, yet the Asian American critique of citizenship generated by its specific history opens the space for such cross-race and cross-national possibilities. One of the important *acts* that the immigrant performs is breaking the dyadic, vertical determination that situates the subject in relation to the state, building instead horizontal community with and between others who are in different locations subject to and subject of the state."[52] *Native Speaker* dramatizes a similar Asian American critique of citizenship through Kwang's political vision, but Lee does not shy away from depicting the near impossibility of achieving such a reality.

Kwang's alternative vision of what Lowe has called a "horizontal community" resonates with Lee's allusions to Walt Whitman throughout the novel; Liam Corley argued that Lee "revises Whitman's heritage of representative Americanness to include the immigrant experience as central."[53] Whitman in fact has the first words of the novel as *Native Speaker*'s epigraph is from Whitman's poem "The Sleepers": "I turn but do not extricate myself, / Confused, a past-reading, another, / but with darkness yet." Cowart has parsed the significance of Lee's choice of epigraph: "Whitman's [poem] catalogues a whole world of sleepers (including immigrants, a catalogue within the catalogue), among whom the speaker wanders, perhaps dreaming himself. Here the night figures the unconscious, the unknown, and death. The speaker embarks on a descent into the self and the self's fears of the night in all its guises, literal and metaphorical. These fears are dispelled at dawn as the poet imagines making peace with darkness and waking to fresh purpose, harrowing knowledge now part of his armamentarium."[54] Although John Kwang's "people" are depicted as updated figures from a Whitman poem,[55] the journey through the night that Cowart described is Henry's journey.

Daniel Y. Kim viewed Kwang as a fictional creation that "answers to a certain Asian American political fantasy which was particularly urgent in the late '80s and '90s." However, according to Kim, this fantasy has no precedent for Lee to model other than the African American example: "Despite the novel's insistence on the Korean-ness of the values that shape Kwang's vision, however, its characterization of him relies fundamentally upon a set of protocols drawn from the African American context which determine what attributes a minority political leader would need to possess in order to seem 'authentic.' As forcefully as the novel might seem to argue for a new 'syntax,' it actually suggests the impossibility of a racial politics that does not frame itself—at least to a significant degree—in the old one."[56] In Kwang's charismatic persona—particularly in his powerful vernacular speeches—Kim has seen the influence of generations of African Americans' political work, not a new model for imagining a political success that deviates from the black-white binary.

Kim also noted that the lack of modeling for imagining a Korean American politician is echoed in the lack of literary modeling; so Lee turns to African American literary precedents and bears a particularly large debt of influence to Ralph Ellison's *Invisible Man*.[57] The lack of a long tradition of Asian American literature, however, is also the source of a major difference between the two novels. Ellison is preoccupied with the failures of past African American movements, while "*Native Speaker* acknowledges that there is no comparably monumental Asian American tradition of political and literary representation upon which to look back. So instead, Lee seems to look forward, to gesture toward the emergence of a new racial politics, one attuned to the increasingly *multi*-racial character of the U.S. population."[58] Lee builds from the African American literature tradition because it is the dominant discourse of resistance to white supremacy.

Reading *Native Speaker* in relationship to *Invisible Man* is particularly instructive in both novels' treatments of invisibility. Chen has noted that while Ellison's nameless protagonist is not a literal spy like Henry is, "he shares with Henry a thematic preoccupation with the problems and possibilities of racial in/visibility."[59] For example, Glimmer and Company recalls Monopolated Light and Power from Ellison's novel; both corporations are suggestive of white supremacy. While the Invisible Man is able to leach power from the grid by going underground, Henry bolsters white power in his work for Glimmer. Henry's invisibility is Hoagland's advantage in their work: "Just stay in the background. Be unapparent and flat. Speak enough so they can hear your voice and come to trust it, but no more, and no one will think twice about who you are" (44). Like the Invisible Man, Henry cannot be seen as an individual person; unlike Ellison's narrator, Henry has an invisibility that makes him only a "comely shadow who didn't threaten them" (53). Christian Moraru wrote, "A victim of his invisibility, Ellison's hero observes rather defensively, from the outside. Henry has learned how to turn the others' blindness into an advantage, into a profitable cover by smartly juggling his linguistic and 'complexional' faces."[60] While Henry's invisibility may be economically profitable, his invisibility is no less harmful to his psyche.

Although Ralph Ellison is the literary predecessor most often discussed in connection to *Native Speaker,* the title calls immediate kinship to another classic novel, Richard Wright's *Native Son* (1940). Yung-Hsing Wu's "Native Sons and Native Speakers" takes Wright's novel as Lee's more obvious debt of influence. She explained the conceptual connection Lee makes by altering Wright's title for his own book: "Nativity links filiation and speech as conditions of the protagonists' subjectivity: native sons by virtue of their birth, Bigger Thomas and Henry Park are also native speakers. Both speak to the effects of nativity, indicting the pretense with which it confers legitimacy on their ethnic differences only to find them wanting."[61] Lee's fruitful engagement with the giants of African American literature here serves to show the underlying similarity of subject position for those whose "ethnic differences" deny them the privileges of whiteness and therefore true citizenship.

The influence of black political and literary discourse is evident throughout *Native Speaker,* but there are noticeably no significant black characters in the book. Henry's longest direct encounter with a black man is brief; while accompanying Kwang, he encounters an African American customer also named Henry angrily trying to get a refund on a defective watch sold by a Korean merchant. As the son of such a man, Henry could have explained the psychology of the merchant to the other Henry and his understanding of the "coin-small salvation" (188) of his slim profit margins, but he remains silent: "I don't know what stopped me. Maybe there was too much to say. Where to begin?" (185). The doubling of their names suggests commonality, and yet Henry does not speak to bridge the cultural divide, something he is uniquely qualified to do. The critic Caroline Rody argued that this scene reveals the limits of the hopeful, unifying rhetoric of Kwang because, "though *Native Speaker* at times registers a capacity for soaring interethnic vision, one might say that blackness marks the sad incompleteness of its hybridity."[62] As Daniel Y. Kim suggested, the novel puts forth a vision for a "new syntax" but also acknowledges the difficulty of enacting that vision when confronting black identity.[63] Rody further explained: "Despite the cynicism and chagrin with which the novel regards Asian-white relations, the plot places Korean Americans as a group in overt hostilities with African Americans only, while it portrays them performing before whites an assimilist 'perfection' that masks a subtle antagonism—recalling, ironically, the Invisible Man. Its hero locked in ambivalent proximity to whites, *Native Speaker* refrains from approaching the people it invokes as literary fathers, a distance haunted by longing, by guilt, and by violence."[64] While Rody noted the way the plot evades bridging black-Korean conflict, she concluded that Lee's debts of influence to major African American authors such as Ellison and Wright (and white canonical authors such as Whitman) work to counter that lacuna by "sending out filaments of love, longing, respect, and brotherhood . . . it is in the less governed, dreamwork realm of intertextuality that Lee draws sympathetic connections from which his plot demurs."[65] What is not accomplished within the content of the book is evoked in its relationship to other works of great literature. In this way Lee places his work within the larger tradition of American literature, connecting to black and white (male) precedents as serves his point of view, while forging new ground.

Lee's self-conscious use of the language of narrative serves to illuminate and remind readers that the story is being constructed by Henry—and Lee. While Henry is spying on Kwang, Henry's coworker Janice jokingly insists that Henry is secretly a novelist writing a book about the fall of a popular politician, which she imaginatively details. When Henry interrupts that he can "see where this is going," Janice replies, "You can with good stories. . . . A good story will sell, book or movie or man. Political lesson number one" (91). "Good stories" are predictable and familiar. Henry's actual job in this instance is to tell that exact story: "I'd just have to lurk close enough and witness the play of the story as we already knew it" (137).[66] John Kwang's story does follow the expected script for an idealistic American politician: he is ultimately publically disgraced, "his downfall . . . strikingly archetypal in national terms."[67]

Cowart observed the parallels between *Native Speaker* and the classic political novel *All the King's Men,* by Robert Penn Warren. Henry, like Jack Burden, narrates the career of a politician who could have been great but is foiled by human weakness.[68] Henry slowly learns John Kwang's secrets. Some are small; Henry realizes that despite Kwang's family-man persona, he is having an affair with one of his staffers. Some secrets are large; he discovers that Kwang was responsible for having his own headquarters bombed in order to kill Eduardo Fermin, who, like Henry, was spying on Kwang. But it is not murder that leads to Kwang's undoing. In the aftermath of the bombing, the press begins to dig into Eduardo's finances, suspecting a money-laundering ring. Kwang begins to unravel as the press investigates his finances and supporters. While drunk, he crashes his car and nearly kills an undocumented, underage Korean girl, whom the press labels a prostitute. This event clearly parallels Edward Kennedy's accident at Chappaquiddick,[69] but Lee's fictional politician is unable to recover his reputation.

Perhaps because "there is something universally chilling about a new plot," Henry does not break from his role in this predetermined play despite his deeply ambivalent feelings for Kwang. Because his job is "to extend the evening's narrative to its logical and fitting end," Henry knows that his work is not simply to record Kwang's actions but to participate in his downfall: "A good spy is but the secret writer of all moments imminent" (198). A spy is a writer, and a writer creates meaning. This metafictional discourse, with Henry's interest in genre and plot, ultimately poses questions about free will and individual agency against the predetermined narrative structures that might decide a person's fate. Is it possible for Kwang to break away from the familiar plot of American politics? Is corruption a necessary part of playing the game of American politics? Is Henry to blame for his complicity in Kwang's fall? Does his betrayal of Kwang constitute a betrayal of his family? Of his heritage?

Yoonmee Chang argued that Kwang's fall is the result of his deviation from the expected roles of Korean Americans in society. Much as Henry suggests that his parents would think Kwang a fool for overstepping his success as a businessman to step into the political realm and that his doom was inevitable, Chang argued that belief in "small business ownership as a route to upward mobility" is a "form of class containment and discipline": "It evinces a reconfiguration of our contemporary racial equilibrium in which racialized subjects are conceded economic advancement as a literal buy off for quiescence in social and political domains." She read Kwang as revealing that "Korean Americans cannot, it turns out, author their subjectivity beyond their culturalizations."[70] Race will determine social position, whether you assimilate or not, Chang has suggested.

There is plenty of blame and guilt for Henry to take on in the course of the narrative. Cowart saw parallels between Lee's narrator and F. Scott Fitzgerald's morally "compromised" narrator Nick Carraway, but he read Henry as "capable of more ethical behavior" despite his new recognition of his moral culpability and—painfully enough—how his moral failings make him a "true American" after all.[71] His "American" identity emerges in his break with Kwang, his substitute Korean father figure, through his parsing of language. Henry narrates the bombing of Kwang's campaign headquarters in the language of language. He notes that in his business, bombing is meant to send messages by "employing a more complicated grammar than is required" (265). Although Henry suspects that Kwang is behind the bombing that killed his fellow spy Eduardo Fermin and the innocent janitor Helda Brandeis, he wishes that Kwang would speak to him in Korean, "by which real secrets may be slowly courted, slowly unveiled" (275).

But it is Kwang's increasing use of Korean and his lapses into accented English that signal his decline. In a press conference after the bombing, Kwang's "voice cracks, and even an accent sneaks through" (293). He gets drunk the night of the car accident and begins to speak Korean to Henry, as the two men dance around the truth of Kwang's guilt. The two men become increasingly aggressive until Kwang confesses, begging Henry to say that he (and "the world") knows that Kwang would undo the murders if possible. Henry does not speak. This recalls their earlier conversation about Kwang's inability to speak out about Eduardo's death without it becoming a racial matter. The racialization of Kwang's reaction is unavoidable. Here, Henry's choice to stay silent when asked to forgive Kwang is the decisive break between them, even as Henry regrets the loss of Kwang's ability to be "effortlessly Korean, effortlessly American" and "the hope of his identity, which may also be mine" (328). Silence too carries depth of meaning.

Jonathan Arac pointed out that criticism of *Native Speaker* often overlooked the fact that Henry does not act on his knowledge of Eduardo's death even though Henry's story is an act of "truth-telling."[72] This, Arac suggested, makes Henry's narrative a public confession.[73] If we view Henry's story as a public act that breaks the silence with which Henry first greeted Kwang's plea for forgiveness, he is granting a sort of absolution by explaining Kwang's psychology to the world. While Henry was once unable to explain the psychology of Korean shopkeepers to the other Henry, he is able to reveal the complexities of Kwang through writing on a much larger scale through this narrative.

Whether telling the truth through confessional narrative is enough to absolve Henry of his complicity in concealing the murders is another question. After Eduardo's death, Henry visits the Fermin family to deliver ten thousand dollars in cash on behalf of John Kwang. Henry takes on the job of mitigating Kwang's guilt, but when Mr. Fermin mistakes Henry for Kwang, the doubling reminds us that it is Henry's guilt too. He covers for Kwang here and does not tell Lelia the truth of what he knows about the bombing despite his claims of finally coming clean to her about his life. He admits that in the past he might have "presented the fact solely to mitigate the ill sweep of my own activities," but he goes only so far to suggest that he might eventually tell her when any potential danger has passed (313). While not owning the full extent of his complicity, Henry casts this decision as not self-serving, as he is not manipulating the narrative to his advantage. A sort of "imperfect" truth, with perhaps an "impure" grace, is the most the reader hopes for Henry.

The first word on the list that Lelia leaves for Henry at the beginning of the novel is that he is "surreptitious" (5), and the novel ends with another list that fulfills that first accusation: Henry takes over Eduardo's job of compiling the personal information of every constituent who donates money to Kwang. While the press interprets the money Kwang receives as suspect (many of his supporters are undocumented), Henry views it as an expanded version of the *ggeh* that gave his father his start in business: "The larger ggeh depend solely on this notion, that the lessons of the culture will be stronger than a momentary lack" (279–80). Narkunas wrote, "Kwang's *ggeh* represents an alternative mode of organization based on networks of possible connections rather than an affective relationship of trust, honor, duty, debt, or heroic agency."[74] Kwang's *ggeh* is idealistic, expanding beyond Korean cultural ties to include anyone needing the safety net and promise of a community. But, as Song argued, "the kind of diaspora implicit to the functioning of *ggeh* does not decline simply because these lives have ceased to experience tragic events. . . . Material success and new social contacts have, in other words, made it difficult to imagine such tragedies as contiguous with group-defining, historically traumatic events."[75] Henry hands over this list to Hoagland, who, he belatedly realized, wanted it from the start. The Immigration and Naturalization Service rounds up three dozen undocumented families from the list, and there is a nativist outcry against Kwang.

Caroline Rody called Henry's work an "ethnic treason."[76] In handing over the list that leads to deportations for fellow neo-Americans, Henry performs his deepest betrayal because he knows their stories since they are his own (260). Moreover, Christian Moraru argued that this type of "self-betrayal" is "part and parcel of immigration and acculturation to the extent that these entail active self-forgetting and self-remaking."[77] It is Henry's success as an American that is the betrayal and, in some respects, could be no other way. His assimilation comes at the cost of renouncing his immigrant roots. This is why Henry wishes for his father's forgiveness, "for what I have done with my life is the darkest version of what he only dreamed of" (334). Crystal Parikh argued that Lee does not excuse Henry for his actions despite his ignorance of Hoagland's endgame.[78] The community of immigrants that Henry betrays is not unified because of the differences among the people Kwang hoped to bridge: "The political invisibility and voicelessness of this population is largely an effect of the language barrier. . . . These recent immigrants remain voiceless because they register each other's differences over affinities, they feel no sense of shared fate with one another, and they possess little or no political knowledge."[79]

Henry does feel affinity across racial and ethnic lines, showing deep understanding and sympathy for fellow outsiders. While he suggests that "have mercy" should be the first words new immigrants learn, he does not show any mercy when it matters most. Henry sees this guilt as part of his "American education" (320): "My ugly immigrant's truth, as was his, is that I have exploited my own, and those others who can be exploited. This forever is my burden to bear. But I and my kind possess another dimension. We will learn every lesson of accent and idiom, we will dismantle every last pretense and practice you hold, noble as well as ruinous. You can keep nothing safe from our eyes and ears. This is your own history" (319–20). Echoing James Weldon Johnson's *The Autobiography of an Ex-Colored Man* (1912), Henry's speech resonates with that novel's narrator's lament that he has sold out his heritage by passing for white to avoid the effects of racism. Lee makes explicit that his narrator's guilt reflects the guilt of the larger nation in demanding immigrant assimilation to a system of racist exploitation. In his switch to a direct address to the reader, he implicates his audience in the collective guilt of American history.

By confronting this truth, Henry frees himself to walk away from Glimmer and Company. He reaches a tentative reconciliation with Lelia in the role of "long-term guest" in their apartment (347). Now jobless, Henry helps Lelia with her speech-therapy work in the public schools. Despite his painful past experience in ESL, he enjoys his work, playing the role of the "Speech Monster" in a green mask while assisting Lelia with the games and activities she designed (348). Henry appears to be finding peace with the past by turning the torture of his childhood language acquisition into a gentle, more inclusive way to teach English. The final scene of the novel has divided critical interpretations. While Tina Chen pointed to Henry's Speech Monster costume as indicative of an ambiguous resolution in Henry's quest for a stable identity,[80] David Cowart read Henry's "understated vision of service" as Henry's only possible source of salvation from existential angst.[81]

Both Min Hyoung Song and Jodi Kim read the conclusion of the novel as Henry's silenced withdrawal into his white wife's domestic space.[82] Sami Ludwig agreed that there is only a private resolution rather than a public one, but she argued that a private resolution is the only real possibility for the problems Lee examines: "This is the therapy of respectful, human change, one that knows about the dangers of language domination and language loss, and of personal caring which requests that the other be encountered at the individual level. . . . the only site where human agency can cultivate any kind of human healing."[83] Ludwig saw healing exemplified in Henry's interaction with Lelia's students: "a vision of hope that the natural abilities of one child gone can survive in other children." Henry picks up the children and feels them to be "a weight so wondrous to me, and awful" (349). He tells them he will miss them when they leave and in doing so says goodbye to his son by proxy. Henry's silent grief finds indirect expression at last.

Henry's presence also serves to validate the students as American. When he takes off his monster mask, the children show "some wonder in their looks as they check again that my voice moves in time with my mouth, truly belong to my face" (349). Henry's role in the classroom unsettles the power dynamics of the classroom that once dominated him, as Henry is fully aligned with neither the teacher nor the students.[84] Lelia too works to dismantle the power that her position as native white schoolteacher could give her: "She wants them to know that there is nothing to fear, she wants to offer up a pale white woman horsing with the language to show them it's fine to mess it all up" (349). Elda E. Tsou noted that Lee's emphasis on Lelia's race here works to make whiteness "visible," so that whiteness is affirmed as nonnative, opening up the possibilities for who qualifies for citizenship.[85] She argued further that Lelia is actually the native speaker of the title who, "once identified with a normative referentiality, is now a figure of other speaking."[86]

In the final lines of the novel, Lelia provides each student with a sticker because each "has been a good citizen," and she calls out their names: "Now, she calls out each one as best as she can, taking care of every last pitch and accent, and I hear her speaking a dozen lovely and native languages, calling all the difficult names of who we are" (349). Parikh read this moment as "an interpellation of the students as American in the name of a radically democratic impulse."[87] Moraru saw Lee celebrating "Whitmanesque heterogeneity," with Lelia realizing "all the idiom's voices and hypostases that she does not fully occupy and in which others can make themselves at home."[88] Lelia's relinquishment of her privilege, as a teacher, as a white woman, as a native speaker, is the prerequisite for successfully incorporating new citizens into America. She does not replicate the trauma of Henry's experience of acculturation; instead she puts forth effort to learn names, to learn to pronounce other languages. While Henry may never make complete peace with his divided identity, Lelia makes it possible for the next generation to find a more comfortable place in the language and in the country.[89] Breaking down normative whiteness, Lee suggests, is the first step in making room for all voices.

CHAPTER 3

"The basic mode of wartime"
A Gesture Life (1999)

As is the case with *Native Speaker,* Chang-rae Lee's second novel, *A Gesture Life,* is told through an unreliable narrator. Franklin "Doc" Hata tells two stories: one about his harrowing experiences in the Japanese military during World War II and another about his quiet postwar suburban life in the United States. Like Henry Park, Hata tells his story as a sort of indirect and evasive confession of his sins. In telling the story of his youth, Hata often distances himself from his younger incarnation by using the third person to narrate his own life and feelings. He begins one sentence with the following: "But if I can speak for that young man now, if I can tell some part of the truth for him . . ." (*A Gesture Life* 240). Disassociating from his own history, Hata attempts to understand what he did and who he was as a way of figuring out who he has become in the decades since the war. The problem is that Hata does indeed only "tell some part of the truth"; his narration frequently avoids full responsibility for his actions. By piecing together what Hata keeps unsaid throughout the course of his story, readers realize the ways his war-time experiences as a medic caring for so-called Korean "comfort women" haunt him as he attempts to repress his memories by devoting himself to American assimilation. In her review of the novel, Michiko Kakutani wrote that "belonging and assimilation come at a cost—in Hata's case, the cost of self-knowledge and genuine emotional connection."[1] In his pursuit of the American dream, he adopts a Korean child as a way to participate in typical suburban life and to ameliorate his feelings of guilt, only to reenact his war-time failures with his adopted daughter. Hata's relationships with women throughout his life reflect the author's critique of paternalism as a means of asserting personal and political dominance.

In praise of the novel, many critics have compared Lee's emotionally disengaged narrator to Kazuo Ishiguro's repressed English butler in *The Remains of the Day* (1989). Lee has cited Ishiguro as well as the novelist Yukio Mishima as influences.[2] The impact of John Cheever on Lee's vision of suburban New York life is also unmistakable; Cheever's 1964 short story "The Swimmer" is referenced early in the novel and lays some of the groundwork for Doc Hata's existential angst. Most often, however, academic critics have compared Lee's depiction of the Korean women held in sexual slavery by the Japanese army during World War II to that in Nora Okja Keller's 1997 *Comfort Woman,* her novel about a former "comfort woman" and her relationship with her daughter.[3] The critic Suk Koo Rhee argued that Lee's novel has been better received in part because of the aesthetics of his "charming sensually attractive work" as compared to Keller's "bare, unbeautiful ethnic material"; the lyricism of Lee's prose, in contrast to Keller's stark style, alters the way readers perceive these authors' treatments of the same traumatic source material.[4] Belinda Kong was more pointed in her comparison by suggesting that Lee "avoids sensationalizing sexual violence" whereas Keller's novel contains "lurid episodes," but the style of Lee's narration also minimizes the brutality of Hata's actions.[5] What these different comparisons highlighted about Lee's novel is his intentional distancing of Doc Hata's narration from the brutality of his war-time experience.[6]

Initially, Lee tried to write the book from the perspective of the comfort women, and he went to South Korea to interview survivors. After writing most of this version of the book, however, he changed course. In a *New York Times* interview with Dwight Garner, Lee explained why he abandoned the project: "I began to feel that what I had written didn't quite come up to the measure of what I had experienced, sitting in a room with these people. I began to feel that there was nothing like live witness."[7] Instead, Lee decided to write "the perpetrator's tale" to explore not how victims move forward but how criminals carry on and live with their actions.[8] Lee's choice to move from direct to indirect representation of these war crimes creates the most compelling drama of the novel, but he reported in *Vulture* that he had to go into therapy after completing the novel "because the narrator of that book is a monster."[9]

The critic Hamilton Carroll argued that the narrative is Hata's effort at bildungsroman; by telling his story, Hata attempts to illustrate his assimilation and thereby prove his citizenship. His effort fails, however, because it is really a trauma narrative that reveals how he has not truly assimilated. Carroll suggested that it is this authorial undercutting of Hata's account that shows how Lee is disrupting the typical form of immigrant literature in which assimilation and belonging are successful.[10] The critic Betsey Huang, however, argued against Carroll's label of bildungsroman and instead asserted that the novel is truly in the form of Hata's memoir: "In this story of remembrance by a man who, in taking stock of his life as an immigrant-cum-American after his retirement, finds that he has lived a life governed by narratives scripted by others, Lee puts the aesthetics of life writing in service of a politics of resistance. As such, *A Gesture Life* is a meta-critique of the hegemonic power of the grand narratives and national romances that undergird assimilationism."[11] Taking care to complicate this vision of the resistant powers of the memoir, Huang noted that "a memoir can commodify traumatic events from far-flung places for vicarious consumption. The genre, then, is imbued with recuperative/liberatory *as well as* prescriptive/coercive capacities, both of which may play a deterministic role in the construction of the immigrant subject."[12] These divergent interpretations of the novel's genre highlight the author's insistence on double reading: Doc Hata's narration should be read critically, with an eye toward the character's intentions in contrast to Lee's larger authorial aims.

The title of the novel cues the reader to Hata's unreliability. *A Gesture Life* begins with Doc Hata's assertions of belonging to "a picturesque town that I will call Bedley Run, [where] I somehow enjoy an almost Oriental veneration as an elder" (1). Although he claims to identify strongly with the locale, the unreliability of the town's actual name (which he admits was changed to sound more affluent) makes this claim suspect. His position as venerated "Oriental" too is unsettling when we learn that most of the local Chinese and African American populations live elsewhere. Despite the clear segregation of his town, Hata insists that he is not "unwelcome" (3). The owner of a medical-supplies business and a stately Tudor revival home, Hata relishes his status as the "model minority" of his community. The critic Sze Wei Ang argued that Hata's model minority status allows him to fixate on his status as an ideal citizen, a strategy which erases his past as an ethnic Korean and as a Japanese veteran even as he becomes "a generic Asian American."[13] To be visibly Asian American is still to be racially marked, but it is not the same as being identified by a specific culture or history. Hata's seemingly privileged status allows him the illusion of belonging even as it obliterates his painful history. While feigning engagement and connection to his community, Doc Hata is really going through the motions of living; his description of his hometown reveals that behind the facade of acceptance, his presentation of his life is out of touch with reality.

Erasing this past is key to Hata's project of rebuilding his sense of his own character. Ang further argued, "For him, racial belonging is premised on the idea of moral goodness, but ironically, he unintentionally decenters this dictum. As Hata understands it, ethics depends upon economic utility, and it is an economic utility that is precariously linked to his status as a racialized subject. Hata's own understanding of his life as meaningful depends on two central aspects of being a model minority: first, through economic success and material wealth . . . , and second, through the figuration of the racial body within the political and civic landscape of the United States."[14] By achieving financial success and becoming the successful "model minority," Hata performs "moral goodness," but as his story unfolds, his claims to such reveal the extent to which the construction itself is ethically bankrupt.

Despite his opening claim that "people know me here," Hata lacks genuine emotional connections to those in his community. Upon arrival in Bedley Run, he realizes that the "worst wrong is to be drawn forth and disturbed," and his knowing assessment of the correct level of neighborly disengagement quickly makes clear that he, as the "interloper," will not trespass on neighborhood privacy (44). His personal relationships, as a result, remain limited. He is friendly with a real estate agent named Liv Crawford, who desperately wants to sell his house.[15] When Hata sets his house on fire while burning personal papers, Liv saves Hata—and the desirable house—from destruction. Because he is estranged from his daughter, Sunny, it is Liv, Liv's former boyfriend Renny, and the hospital staff who visit him in the hospital. In his conversation with Renny we learn that Hata once had a girlfriend named Mary Burns, who had been significant in his life. Mary had died the previous year of liver cancer, and yet Hata had not visited her in the hospital before her death for fear of upsetting her with their past history. Hata is hesitant to offer himself emotionally throughout the novel, as when he learns that Patrick Hickey, the son of the couple to whom he sold his medical-supply business, is waiting for a heart transplant within the same hospital. Knowing that the business is failing and that Mrs. Hickey would like to visit her son with Hata, he still does not seek her out. His fear of emotional entanglements outweighs his sense of sympathy and desire to connect. While the isolation of Hata's life is chilling, Aliki Varvogli wrote, "the otherness he carries within him does not mark him as not belonging; rather, it describes him perfectly as an American citizen in the late twentieth century, a rootless man dislocated at home."[16]

In an interview in *The Very Telling,* Lee explained the significance of Hata's desire to assimilate even as he keeps his distance from the community:

> There's a deep-seated human need to assimilate and be part of a group. It's a survival technique. We all talk about being individuals, especially in this country, but really we're not. We're members of many different little groups. For an outsider like an immigrant, the idea is not to stand out because when you stand out you get cut down. To be an individual is to be in a dangerous position. It's about the overriding desire to join, but then in most of that book, and especially in *A Gesture Life,* it's about the darker side of

> assimilation and what people become when they've given up themselves. This invisibility is self-imposed, not like the invisibility of Ralph Ellison, which is imposed from the outside. This invisibility I'm writing about is a kind of self-protection, but it's not without ill effect.[17]

Hata's acceptance of his designated role as the "model minority" is an acceptance of the sort of invisibility that Lee described. In this role he is safe, free from the difficulties of real personal relationships—and free to keep his past a secret. But this status comes at the cost of isolation.

The details of his relationships with the people in Bedley Run reveal that Doc Hata is not an entirely innocent believer in the myth of the American dream as he so staunchly insists. His decision to sell his business to the Hickeys, for example, occurred shortly before a recession that he foresaw, and he kept his concerns about their ability to meet their mortgage payments to himself. Although presented as a desire not to overstep politeness, this silence financially benefited Hata. His own business success, in turn, is revealed to be due in part to the intercession of Mary Burns with the local bank on his behalf—a fact that Sunny remembers even if her father downplays this action in his own memory. His financial success was not self-made despite his hard work and his belief in the bootstrap opportunities that America provides.

His friendships with other Asian Americans also reveal the extent to which Hata's proclamations do not match reality, particularly in his awareness of his own racial difference in the community. He remembers a time when he failed to befriend a Japanese American he met at a convention: "I first wondered if he felt he wasn't Japanese enough for me, or whether I thought myself not American enough for him. But later on, after returning home, I thought perhaps it was that we felt different from everyone by virtue of being together (these two Japanese in a convention crowd), and that it was this fact that made us realize, for a moment, our sudden and unmistakable sense of not fitting in" (20). Hata's discomfort at being seen with another Japanese American highlights his position in his home community not only as the model minority but also as the isolated exception to the dominant whiteness of the town. He feels his difference more pointedly when he is with another Asian American. While Hata's discomfort reveals the limitations of embracing the model minority paradigm as an Asian American, he is determined to play this part regardless of his reception.

Unlike the Japanese American businessman, Renny is East Indian and not East Asian, which helps Hata feel more comfortable in their difference. Although he is "East Indian of blood," Renny Banerjee is described by Hata "as a very American sort of man" (37). Renny too is Asian American, but Hata stresses Renny's American-ness, showing that Hata does have an understanding of American belonging that goes beyond racial identification alone. Although Renny seems more American than Asian to Hata, Renny's racial consciousness is far more astute than his friend's. Renny, noticing the way people in the town have begun to make racial remarks openly in his presence, feels anger. Hata replies that "the predominant burden is mine, if it is a question of feeling at home in a place. . . . If people say things, I try not to listen. In the end, I have learned I must make whatever peace and solace of my own" (135). While this appears to be a pat statement of the immigrant's responsibility to adapt to the United States, the absurdity of feeling at home by ignoring racial slurs helps the reader see the artifice of Hata's home in Bedley Run.

The facade of "peace and solace" that Doc Hata has found in Bedley Run shows further cracks as his references to memories of the past and his estranged daughter, Sunny, become more frequent in the narrative. Significantly, the first reference to Hata's adopted daughter comes shortly after he has casually denied his relationship to her in a conversation with Mrs. Hickey. Rather than acknowledge Sunny as his child, he implies that she was an exchange student who "came from Japan . . . many years ago, and stayed for some schooling" (13). Beyond the obvious horror of not recognizing Sunny as his daughter, his fiction that Sunny, a Korean orphan, is Japanese resonates with his initial desire to adopt a Japanese girl. This preference is tied to Hata's own history as an adopted child. The son of ethnic Koreans living in a ghetto in Japan, Hata, whose full birth name is never given, was adopted by a wealthy Japanese family and renamed Jiro Kurohata. While Hata professes gratitude to both his birth and adopted families, he feels that it was ultimately "the purposeful society" of Japan that truly raised him. By adopting a child from Japan, Hata would be honoring his parent country and returning the gift that he feels Japan gave to him.

Despite his initial preference, Hata accepted Sunny when no Japanese orphans were available. The critic Jenny Wills argued that "by adopting a child from Korea, Hata participates in this [U.S.] national acceptance of responsibility for those orphaned children" created as a result of the Korean War. In accepting Sunny, however, Hata's hopes for a child of "like-enough race" (73) were dashed when he saw her for the first time:

> I instantly saw in my mind the picture of her at the age when she first came to me. A skinny, jointy young girl, with thick, wavy black hair and dark-hued skin. I was disappointed initially; the agency had promised a child from a hardworking, if squarely humble, Korean family who had gone down on their luck. . . . But of course I was over-hopeful and naïve, and should have known that he or she would likely be the product of a much less dignified circumstance, a night's wanton encounter between a GI and

> a local bar girl. I had assumed the child and I would have a ready, natural affinity, and that my colleagues and associates and neighbors, though knowing her to be adopted, would have little trouble in quickly accepting our being of a single kind and blood. But when I saw her for the first time I realized there could be no such conceit for us, no easy persuasion. Her hair, her skin, were there to see, self-evident, and it was obvious how some other color (or colors) ran deep within her. And perhaps it was right from that moment, the very start, that the young girl sensed my hesitance, the blighted hope in my eyes. (204)

Hata's disappointment in Sunny's visible African American lineage has disrupted his fantasy of a racial affinity that could disguise the fact that Sunny is adopted; he had hoped their racial difference in a predominately white town would unify them as a family in the eyes of the community. Instead, Hata's own racial biases have created a barrier to forging a genuine relationship with his adopted daughter.[18] Although Sunny cries upon arrival at her new home, Hata comforts her in English, not Korean, though it was his first language as well. Instead of building upon this common ground to become a real father to Sunny and ease her transition, Hata throws himself into home improvement projects. Because adopting Sunny becomes another marker of his own racial difference in the community, Hata reinvests himself in performing wealth through the beautification of his home.

Hata's reaction to Sunny's miscegenated body represents "U.S. colonialism in Korea, and the failure of Asian sovereignty is metonymically read as the failure of Japanese imperialism."[19] This association reminds him of the Japanese defeat in World War II and the end of Japanese occupation in Asia, and though he is ethnically Korean, the end of Japanese domination haunts him even as his participation in the imperial project has warped his psyche.[20] The critic Mark C. Jerng argued that "just when he thinks he can erase his own participation in the Japanese army's imperial efforts by adopting and forging a natural father-daughter relationship with a Korean girl, another history of war and occupation, the US role in the Korean war, emerges in the very place of that erasure."[21] Having replaced one imperial national identity with another, Hata is left to confront Sunny's body as a sign of American colonialism, and as Belinda Kong argued, "unbeknownst to Hata, it is this neocolonial attitude of paternalism and control that makes him most American."[22]

His preoccupation with Sunny's body manifests itself as well in his preoccupation with her sexuality. Beautiful and rebellious, teenaged Sunny asserts her autonomy by running away from home and moving into the house of a notorious drug dealer named Jimmy Gizzi. After waiting three weeks for Sunny to return, Hata seeks her out at Gizzi's house, where a wild party is under way. Stumbling across a couple having sex in an upstairs bedroom, Hata is convinced that the woman is Sunny, and he feels repulsed at her "carnality" and wishes she were "nothing to me" so that he could attack the couple with the small knife he carries for protection (104). Although the woman turns out not to be Sunny, Hata's reaction to the supposed sight of his daughter is extreme and disturbing. The violence of Hata's reaction is at this point in the novel confounding because the reader does not yet know the nature of his past, but this encounter with "Sunny's" sexuality takes Hata immediately into memories of his time in the army during World War II when a young prostitute jumped to her death in Singapore. Hata views his adopted daughter's sexuality through the lens of his war-time experience. Suk Koo Rhee observed that the narrative connection that Hata draws between the comfort woman and Sunny is meant to "slander an interracial relationship by lumping it together with his memories of war crimes," thus making Sunny's consensual partner a rapist.[23]

Hata's concern may be read as the protective gesture of a traumatized father, but this interpretation is too pat to encompass the complexity of Hata's sense of sexuality and his own guilt.[24] Although he warns Sunny that women who leave their homes "would inevitably descend to the lowest level of human society and be forced to sell every part of themselves, in mind and flesh and spirit" (144), his admonition shows as much victim blaming as fatherly concern. When Sunny confesses to having been attacked by Gizzi, Hata's immediate response is "This is what happens when you offer yourself so freely" (149). Sunny, however, refuses to accept blame for her own victimization. She further declares that she would commit suicide before ever letting herself be raped. Shocked by Sunny's confession, Hata is more disturbed by the connection of Sunny's threat to "a long-stored memory of another young woman who once spoke nearly the same words" (150). Sunny's sexuality and victimization prompt Hata to recall his role as a medic for the forced prostitutes during the war in Burma and Kkutaeh, the dead "comfort woman" whom he once claimed to love.[25] Jerng noted that the way the narrative moves back and forth between memories of different times and places operates as a "model of transference."[26] Invoking Jacques Lacan, Jerng argued that "the repetition of transference does not repair the past relationship so much as it repeats what was repressed in the past relationship."[27] If Hata is unconsciously repeating his history with Kkutaeh in his relationship with Sunny, it is not a recuperative act of memory but in fact a barrier to facing the truth of his relationship with Kkutaeh. Kong suggested that in adopting Sunny, Hata was desiring "not so much K resurrected as K reincarnated in purer, virginal form" and that "this adoption fantasy may be read as another symptom of Hata's criminal repression, another obliquely calculated move of his unconscious to repair his loss of and appease his guilt over K."[28]

Like his later incarnation's devotion to being the ideal American citizen, young Hata as Jiro Kurohata is deeply invested in performing his role as an ideal imperial Japanese soldier. Determined to perform his "duty for Nation and Emperor" as a field medic, Jiro hopes to "prove to anyone who might suspect otherwise the worthiness of raising me away from the lowly quarters of my kin and reveal the essential, inner spirit that is within us all" (120).[29] Jiro's dedication to his profession is part of his project of proving himself worthy of his adoption.[30] To that end, he sets up his de facto commanding officer, the sadistic Japanese doctor Captain Ono, as a role model to follow. In one of Hata's first flashbacks, he recalls Ono's repeatedly stopping and restarting the heart of a condemned Burmese prisoner who was only mildly sedated. The scene is a horrifying example of medical torture, and yet Hata blandly recalls that "to me it seemed more academic than anything else" (76). Blinded by Ono's "elite caste" and social position, Jiro Kurohata accepts the captain's war crime without moral judgment.

Jiro's response to the torture of the Burmese man helps put his cold bureaucratic response to the conditions of the "comfort women" in perspective with what Hannah Arendt famously called "the banality of evil."[31] When he is first stationed in Singapore, a newly arrived Korean sex slave begs Hata to help her. He replies in Korean only, "There's no place to go" (111). His matter-of-fact acceptance of her captivity results in his complicity, as he hands the girl over to the officer from whom she was fleeing. Despite his own professed disgust at prostitution, Hata resists any sentimentality for his Korean heritage and affirms the Japanese order. This behavior continues when five young Korean women are shipped to Burma to "service" Hata's camp. Euphemistically calling the young women "female volunteers," he recommends that a sex-obsessed corporal make use of the women, so long as the corporal remembers his "dignity" in service to the empire (162). Corporal Endo becomes increasingly agitated and refuses his place in the "lottery" that determines when he may visit the "comfort station." Hata watches from afar as a "disinterested spectator" and sees Endo grab one of the girls and drag her finto the bushes (187). Endo, however, slits the girl's throat rather than raping her. Charged with treason instead of murder, Endo is beheaded as punishment for having "stolen or despoiled the camp's armament or rations" (189). The death of the young girl is notable to those in charge only as a loss of property, not as a loss of life. For all its perversity, Endo's murder of the girl could be seen as an act of mercy: he saves her from torture and possibly a prolonged death. Endo, unlike Hata, questions the morality of using Korean women as sex slaves and rebels against authority even though his act costs him his life. Whether motivated by pity or shame, however, Endo too takes agency away from his victim.

The victim's sister, Kkutaeh (whom Hata tellingly reduces to only K), does view Endo's action as a mercy. When Captain Ono takes a special interest in K, Hata is made responsible for treating her for disease and delivering her to Ono whenever he has hung a black flag to summon her. This flag serves as an insult to Hata as well by reminding him of his second-class status in Japanese society; his Japanese family name means "black flag," an ancient symbol of "contagion" (224). With K under Hata's supervision, he learns that K is not only happy for her sister but also wishes for the same fate, and she begs Hata "as a countryman" to kill her (238). When he refuses, she strategically attacks him, but Hata only knocks her unconscious. When she wakes, she vows to kill herself before she allows Ono to hurt her, and Hata feels a "certain connection" to K as "any young man might naturally feel for a young woman" (239). The situation, of course, is not natural, and he frequently overlays the rhetoric of romance over their encounters. His response to his violence is to feel love for his victim, a reaction that suggests love of power more than love of K as a person. The critic Anne Anlin Cheng wrote, "In light of K's captivity, the question of her consent in this 'courtship' can only be a false one. Declaring his sincere intentions in ways at once conventional and elliptical, Hata's words fold rape into love, strain into promise, highlighting the disturbing gap *and* intimacy between rhetoric and reality, between romance and coercion. The universalizing language of romance here authorizes forms of violence and domination."[32] Although he is her captor, Hata likens their conversations to "an initial date, like any two university students" (248). While Hata evades the reality of his relationship with the enslaved K, the reader is unable to forget her vulnerability.

Because the novel is told only from Hata's perspective, it is impossible to read Kkutaeh's version of events, but by reading Hata's narrative with suspicion, it is possible to interpret Kkutaeh's motivations as we learn more about her. Kkutaeh, whose name means "bottom, or last," is from an elite Korean family whose patriarch, like Hata, advocated pan-Asian unity against the West (173). While Hata is pleased with this parallel to the emperor's mandate, K is quick to suggest that this philosophy only privileges the Japanese empire. More politically astute than Hata, she quickly changes the subject to that of European novels, promising to play along with Hata's fantasy of romance—so long as he recognizes this as fantasy. The critic Kandice Chuh has read Hata's "romance" with K as his parallel romance with Japan. She wrote, "The consequences of the mythification of both nation and woman consequent to this trope are obvious: erasure of complexity and contradiction, the ascription of a fictive unity/purity that cannot and does not exist, and, particularly with the category 'woman,' the effective undermining of an ability to have a standing as a person."[33] Betsey Huang explained how the contradiction of Hata's "romance" with a woman he holds in sexual captivity mirrors his own identity struggle throughout his life:

> Significantly, Lee bifurcates here the romance of heroism into two competing models. On the one hand, Hata reveres the unassailable power that comes with what he sees as the necessary tough love of the Japanese state. . . . On the other hand, he is captivated by a Western romance of liberation in which the oppressed and downtrodden are emancipated by a benefactor of uncommon moral strength. The *sui generis* ideal of the liberation romance thus contradicts the *exemplary* ideal of the "purposeful society"; whereas the former foregrounds an emancipated individual against the tyranny of the state, the latter vests the state with the authority to determine and enforce the roles of its citizens and subjects for the sake and coherency of national identity. The contradiction, while suggesting an Eastern versus Western conception of ideal subjecthood, also lays bare the ways in which both are fully constituted by their own repertoires of nationalistic lore.[34]

Torn between his ambition to prove himself a valuable member of Japanese society by performing his role as medic/captor and his desire to rescue K from her fate, Hata has desires that are in direct contradiction to the world of the Japanese camp in Burma. His conflicting urges play out over this course of his relationship with K. Even after the conclusion of the war and his move to the United States, however, Hata remains torn between this apparent "Eastern vs. Western conception of selfhood." He tries to live out these ideals in each respective culture despite the injustices that these ideologies conceal and perpetuate. This behavior is a conflict of nationalistic mythologies with moral justice that he never fully reconciles as Jiro Kurohata or as Franklin Hata.

Hata's love of K has as much to do with his contradictory identities as an ethnic Korean and a Japanese citizen as with K herself. Hamilton Carroll noted, "Hata's shortening of Kkutaeh to K in his narrative clearly signals his desire to disarticulate their shared ethnic and national heritages and his desire to foreclose the strong identification he feels with K because she is Korean."[35] Chuh has further argued that as K "stands as the logical conclusion of a colonial epistemology that produces the other as the less-than-self, the less-than-human, K also reflects though inexactly Hata's own position as the product of colonialism. To be 'Korean' within this economy is to be the comfort woman; to be 'Japanese' is to be the abuser."[36]

Although he condescendingly dismisses his fellow soldiers' desires for any "brief warm pleasure" as "the basic mode of wartime" (251), Hata's moral high ground and chivalric fantasies give way to violence. He undeniably sides with the abuser in his relationship with K as he rapes her repeatedly but cloaks his abuse in the rhetoric of romance. Shrouding his actions in subtle language, Hata presents this action as "natural" and "chaste" even as it is clear that K feigns sleep and lies immobile beneath him (260). Hata even explains her tears afterward as the result of having lost her virginity. Decades after raping K, Hata is unable or unwilling to confront the reality of his actions. Rhee argued that the narrative's overlay of romantic convention makes the gruesome brutality of history more palatable for readers and conceals the violence of his actions with "a male aestheticism that displaces the reader's attention to these sensory images with their oddly spiritual quality."[37] Hata's strategy for evasion of reality works to temper the reader's response to this brutality as well as assuage the narrator's guilt.

After Hata assaults K, he fantasizes about killing Captain Ono, but he only brings himself to confront the man and confess his love of Ono's special captive. Ono, of course, has anticipated Hata's speech and berates him for his weakness. He then explains that he has singled K out for special attention because of her elite caste; he wants to observe how her superior breeding plays out in her extreme circumstances. Ono then tells Hata that K was already pregnant when Ono first raped her so he has decided to study how long she stays pregnant when transferred back to full duty. Hata confronts K with Ono's story. She denies it, but he assaults her again: "She did not hold me but she did not push me away. I never meant for this but I could no longer balk, or control myself, and then something inside her collapsed, snapped clean, giving way like some storm-besieged roof, and then I descended upon her, and I searched her, every lighted and darkened corner, and every room" (296).[38] K's interior "collapse" is Hata's projection only, and her passive response to his "siege" cannot be viewed as consent. That Hata uses the language of warfare to describe his actions serves to shift blame to circumstance rather than to his own agency. After this assault, Hata overhears Ono speaking to K and realizes "how I must have sounded when I was with her" (296). This moment of recognition leads Hata to feel sorry for Ono when he witnesses his embrace of K. This unexpected identification with Ono supports what Huang has argued is the true motivation for Hata's obsession with K: to be like his idol, Ono.[39]

When the moment comes for Hata to kill Ono, he is unable to do so, thinking only that if Ono were to shoot him, he would then retaliate to "rid her of both of us" (298). K, however, takes the action that Hata cannot and slits Ono's throat with a scalpel. Although he realizes that she should kill him as well, K does not kill Hata for the same reason that she lets him have sex with her: "not for passion or love, or mercy or humanity, but their complete absence and abasement, such that there were no wrongs remaining, no more crimes, nothing to save herself from" (299). Having killed Ono, K refuses to continue Hata's charade that they have a happy future in front of them. In a speech that finally speaks the truth, K reveals her thoughts: "You think you love me but what you really want you don't yet know because you are young and decent. But I will tell you now, it is my sex. The thing of my sex. If you could cut it from me and keep it with you like a pelt or a favorite stone, that would be all. You are a decent man, Lieutenant, but really you are not any different from the rest. I'm sorry I gave myself to you, not for me but for you. Perhaps it was a second's hope. For that I'll be sorry to my death. But if you loved me, Lieutenant, if you truly loved me, you could not bear to be with me. You could not see me like this, you could not stand for one moment longer the thought of my even living" (300). The repetition of "decent" as K vividly describes how Hata has objectified her body underscores just how far from decent he is. Having repeatedly asked Hata to help her commit suicide, K gives Hata one last chance to prove his decency by forcing him to confront the truth: that he desires her body only. There can be no happy outcome to K's story; already marked by her status as a "comfort woman," she will not survive. She asks Hata to kill her for either love or mercy, to act as Corporal Endo did in killing her sister quickly in the clearing away from the camp. Unable to kill K, Hata shoots Ono's corpse to conceal the stab marks and to present Ono's death as suicide.

While Hata conceals his own role in Ono's death, he has not saved K from her death. Another officer, angered at her separation from the rest of the camp, tries to take K back to the comfort house, but she cuts him in a final act of resistance that results in her inevitable death. Although he witnesses K's attack on the officer, Hata is sent to administer sedatives to Colonel Ishii and lingers with his patient long enough for K to be gang raped, murdered, and dismembered by twenty-five or more soldiers. Cheng wrote, "What seems troubling about Hata's choice not to act is not that he could not kill the woman he loved but rather that he never seemed to acknowledge the implications of what his choice meant. In a way, he never made a choice."[40] Yet, Hata did choose to leave K to this brutal fate by not acting at all.

Although Hata does not witness the moment of K's death, he goes to the clearing where K's sister was murdered to find dozens of men covered in gore from K's dismembered corpse. Hata's narration of collecting K's body parts is indistinct and dreamlike: "I could not feel my hands as they gathered, nor could I feel the weight of such remains. And I could not sense that other, tiny, elfin form I eventually discovered, miraculously whole, I could not see the figured legs and feet, the utter, blessed digitation of the hands. Nor could I see the face, the perfected cheek and brow. Its pristine sleep still unbroken, undisturbed. And I could not know what I was doing, or remember any part"

(305). Although Hata narrates this scene with repeated insistence that he "could not" feel, sense, see, or know the truth there, his very recollections here show his words to be wishful thinking. Divorcing himself from the reality of K's obliterated body, he distances himself from this truth that belies his role in it. By focusing on the details of the fetus K carried, Hata also distances K from this memory of collecting her body parts. Suk Koo Rhee argued that in describing K's unborn child, Hata "uses the language of fairy-tale romance," which, again, allows the reader "aesthetic consumptions of the described war crimes."[41] Like Sleeping Beauty, the fetus remains pure and untouched in his imagery despite the rapacious violation of its death. Cheng noted the "lyricism" of this passage and suggested that it reveals "the fracture of Hata's conflicted identifications."[42] Again using the rhetoric of romance that characterizes his narration of his "love" of K to conceal the brutality of Japanese war crimes, Hata has shown that his ultimate affiliation is not with this fantasy plot but with his identification as a Japanese soldier.

Decades after the trauma of this experience, Hata is haunted by K: "And as deeply as I wished she were some wondrous, ethereal presence, that I was being duly haunted, I knew she was absolute, unquestionably real, a once-personhood come wholly into being" (286). K is not merely a spectral presence; Hata is convinced that K is fully embodied in her visitation.[43] Rather than feel fear or remorse at seeing K again, he tries to convince K to be satisfied with "their" life in Bedley Run and to remain with him despite her wish for change. Even after all this time, Hata still wishes to compel K's spirit to follow his wishes. She, of course, disappears, but the spectral K reinforces the image of K that the narrative presents: she is elusive and unreadable. Cheng argued that K "must remain spectral. Her recumbence is the shadow of his subjectivity. The point is not to chide the protagonist in some pious way for not seeing his beloved as a 'real person' but to understand that fetishization may be the form of seeing through the eyes of love."[44]

Critics have disagreed what the impact of K's spectral status has on understanding the "truth" of the narrative. Carroll has argued that though Hata attempts to create his own identity through the denial of subjectivity to the comfort women he treats, the instability of his narration "constitutes the very site of their reenfranchisement as traumatic subjects."[45] Similarly, Christopher Lee suggested that K's reappearance after her death underscores her power: "Even though K's 'haunting' suggests a rupture in the novel's realist commitments, it simultaneously reveals the formal basis of the novel's historicism by suggesting that K cannot be constrained within the materialist parameters of Hata's narrative. This crucial exemption authorizes her indispensable role as the novel's source of objective truth and ethical direction. In short, K enables the text to combine its historicist and political commitments by way of a sublimated identity politics."[46] Both of these readings stress the way Lee undermines Hata's efforts to conceal historical truth.[47] The critic Belinda Kong, on the other hand, argued that this same authorial move on Lee's part "composes the comfort woman figure as a point of unknowability rather than a source of ethnic knowledge. In fact, K's spectral status intimates that ethnic identification in the novel is more uncanny than consolidated, more melancholic than self-validating."[48] In Kong's view, K "materializes only as a sign of the gothic . . . and it leaves the reader with an eerie sense of an event without survivors."[49]

After K's departure, Hata goes to Sunny's old bathroom and fills her tub with hot water after letting the red rust run clear. He submerges himself beneath the water like a fetus, desiring "erasure" if not "innocence" (290). As with his speech to the ghostly K about taking satisfaction with "their" life in Bedley Run, Hata's reaction to K's visit blurs the boundary between his past relationship with K and his present relationship with his daughter. The fetal imagery invokes K's dead infant but also Sunny's. When a seventeen-year-old Sunny became pregnant with her African American boyfriend Lincoln's child, Hata insisted she get an abortion. The reader first learns of Sunny's abortion when she informs her father that she does not blame him for arranging the procedure as they begin to reconcile at the end of the novel. Though introduced as a topic of absolution, Hata admits in the narration—and not to Sunny herself—that he "forced her to do it," knowing how scared and uncertain she was at the time (283). Only at the end of the novel does Hata give the full story of Sunny's abortion. "Too long with child," Sunny is too close to delivery for a legal abortion when she arrives back on Hata's doorstep. Concerned about "only the imminent disgrace and embarrassment that would hang about the house like banners of our mutual failure," Hata ignores Sunny's feelings and charges ahead with a secretive late abortion conducted by an immigrant doctor (340). Worse still, Hata assists the doctor throughout the procedure as Sunny watches them both through her anesthesia. This scene with Sunny echoes two gruesome scenes from Hata's time in Burma: his assistance with Ono's medical experimentation on the prisoner of war and the removal of K's fetus during her murder. Although he vividly remembers, Hata does not narrate these memories in detail; instead he asserts that he should be cast out of society for the things he has witnessed, even as he acknowledges that there has been no punishment for his sins, only "warmth and privilege accruing me unabated, ever securing my good station here, the last place I will belong" (346).

That Sunny and Hata reconcile in immediate juxtaposition to the revelations of the cause of their breach works against a happy conclusion for Hata's story. The object of his redemption comes in the form of Thomas, Sunny's son who is born after her estrangement from Hata. Ever preoccupied by miscegenation, Hata notes that Thomas is of mixed race, but due in part to his long estrangement from Sunny, he embraces his new role as almost grandfather to the boy. The critic Christian Moraru noted that Thomas, unlike the rest of the town, calls Hata "Franklin"—the patriotic name of American individualism and reinvention that Jiro Kurohata takes for himself when coming to the United States—thereby "releasing him" from his former identity.[50]

Although he has a pool of his own, Hata takes Thomas to the public pool in town, where the boy plays with other children and Hata interacts more directly with members of the community. Hata's engagement at the public pool for Thomas's sake is in sharp contrast to the isolation of Sunny's upbringing, and it recalls an early scene in the novel when Hata remembers reading John Cheever's "The Swimmer" in one of Sunny's schoolbooks.[51] He is taken with the conclusion of the story when the swimmer finds himself alone in his own house after swimming across the neighborhood in other people's backyard pools. Hata concludes that the man "ultimately finds himself, if in spiritual disillusion" (23). Afraid at the beginning of the novel that he too could be a "secret swimmer" who remains "silent and unseen" (24), by the conclusion of the narrative, Hata is making efforts to be seen and admits to experiencing finally "the kind of modest, pure joy that comes from something like simply holding Thomas's hand" (333).

In an act that appears to offer Hata a sort of redemption, he saves Thomas and Renny Banerjee from drowning. As with all of Hata's actions, even these acts of heroism are tempered by his decision to save Thomas first even though he is physically closer to Renny,[52] who has had a heart attack while searching for Thomas in the water. Thomas, unlike his multiracial child counterpart Mitt in *Native Speaker*, is saved. Hata finally chooses his family as his first priority. Suk Koo Rhee argued that Hata's acceptance of Thomas reconstructs Hata as "a new minority subject, the kind of model citizen whom the United States desperately needs to restructure its interminority relations."[53] The "new minority subject" described by Rhee still strives for the American dream but no longer uses racism to separate minority communities.

Matthew Miller has argued that the novel ends with "recuperation": by coming to terms with his Korean heritage through his remembrance of K, Hata is able to reconnect to Sunny and reconcile his guilt.[54] This redemptive interpretation, however, does not take into account the ambiguous conclusion to Hata's narrative. Hata's reconciliation with Sunny seems redemptive only if one ignores the ways the novel has refused to endorse Hata's conflation of Sunny and K. Kong has interpreted this scene as less a genuine moral transformation and more a narrative move that turns public shame into private redemption: "We can go further and say that such a recuperative conclusion disquietingly divorces responsibility from the realm of political action and relegates it to that of private conscience—and private penance, after all, is not public reparation. Tellingly, once K has served her textual function as the crime to be pleaded guilty to, the novel transfers Hata's redeeming feats onto other marginalized American subjects as surrogate beneficiaries."[55] His reconciliation with Sunny and the salvation of Thomas and Renny can in no way absolve Hata of his sins against Kkutaeh during the war. The limits of individual grace are called into question in the face of the collective crime of war; only "public reparation," as Kong has termed it, could be the beginning of a path to justice—something that the real comfort women of World War II were largely denied.[56]

In the final passages of the novel, Hata plans to sell his house and use the profits to buy the Hickeys' defaulted mortgage, set aside money for young Patrick's medical treatment, and set Sunny up with a store of her own. But rather than stay and reap the rewards of his benevolent behavior, Hata plans to leave Bedley Run and travel the world: "Let me simply bear my flesh, and blood, and bones. I will fly a flag. Tomorrow, when this house is alive and full, I will be outside looking in. I will be already on a walk someplace, in this town or the next or one five thousand miles away. I will circle round and arrive again. Come almost home" (356). Ultimately, Hata allows for Sunny's family to thrive, but he will not be an active participant in it. He sacrifices his monument to American assimilationism—his suburban house—to become a rootless traveler no longer looking for a place or an affiliation to determine his identity. Huang wrote that in Lee's novel, "the inability to recover a familial—and, I would argue, national—narrative" shows a resistance to the narrative outcome usually demanded "for the American immigrant subject" and "redirects readerly attention to the forces of assimilation and colonialism that fracture and erase such histories."[57]

As in *Native Speaker,* Lee unequivocally rejects the romantic immigrant plot. Carroll noted that the novel's connection of K and Sunny, the daughter of a Korean prostitute, "links the imperialism of Hata's Japanese past to the contemporary conditions of US military imperialism."[58] Yet Kandice Chuh argued that the novel "conceptualizes Korea as *post*colonial rather than *neo*colonial":[59] "The contrast between K and Sunny sediments an understanding of Korea as victim. Beaten and raped, driven to violence herself, K dies. 'K' here easily refers both to this character and to Korea itself. 'Kkutaeh,' meaning the end or the bottom piece, was the name given to her because she was the last of the children born to her family. It bears here even greater resonance as signifying the end of Korea. Sunny, on the other hand, liberated from Doc Hata, from a colonial past, promises and delivers—through Thomas—continuity into the future. Her name baldly gestures toward daybreak, a clearly forward-looking orientation."[60] In Chuh's reading of the novel, Korea is represented as destroyed not by U.S. division of the country but by Japanese colonialism. Sunny, a child of the Korean War, ultimately finds hope and peace in the United States. Kong similarly read the representational politics of geography in the novel: "In Lee's partitioning, Asia stays largely fixed as the space and as the time of war atrocities and biopolitical regimes of death, whereas America signifies the geographical and temporal site of survival and memory, repression and its overturning, guilt and its absolution."[61]

Although she has also denied complete redemption to Hata, Cheng has suggested that at the conclusion of the novel, Hata has moved from "active passivity" to "an active refusal to act further in bad faith" in "recognition of the ethical contamination under which he has been living."[62] "If gesture in the novel had initially stood for empty acts," she wrote, "then what we see at the end of the novel is not a righteous denunciation of those gestures but a refiguring of the very notion of gesture as the form of desire. . . . Hata's final position significantly refuses the complacency of such critical detachment [that would feign the ability to be] an 'objective' witness to the Other."[63] Cheng's interpretation allows us to see Lee's title not as a condemnation of "empty" gestures but instead as signifying hope for moral reckoning, gestures toward good faith and honesty.[64] Perhaps, Lee suggests, moral absolution is impossible for sins of such magnitude, but Hata's act of confession—much like Henry Park's—bears sublimated witness not only to his guilt but also to the larger crimes of cultures bent on domination. Reconciliation, if not justice, begins with recognition, and that may be the hardest task of all.

A Gesture Life deals with many of the same issues as does *Native Speaker:* the difficulties of assimilation; the inability to acknowledge the truth of the self; the damage that emotionally detached masculinity inflicts on women. Lee's second novel, however, takes a far darker path. Readers may be willing to overlook Henry Park's betrayals, but Doc Hata's actions are far greater sins. Unlike Park's struggle to claim an identity, Hata's internalized racism and sense of inferiority, coupled with his narrative denials and evasions, not only threaten his sense of self but also pose actual danger to those in his power. As Hata is caught up in the horrors of war, it is difficult not to attribute his actions to both circumstance and moral failing, and while he wishes for redemption by the conclusion of the novel, it may be impossible. Lee continues to explore characters who undergo moral awakenings in his third novel, *Aloft*. Like Hata and Park, Jerry Battle is emotionally evasive and disconnected from life in a way that reveals his white, masculine privilege. While the stakes of Jerry's actions are not as extreme as Hata's, Jerry too must confront and atone for his failings. Lee's early works suggest that storytelling may be the only way to reexamine a life.

CHAPTER 4

"The last living white man"

Aloft (2004)

Because Lee's third novel is narrated by a white, middle-aged American man and takes place entirely in suburban New York, *Aloft* was initially either critically dismissed as a minor work departing from the expectation that Lee would again represent an Asian American protagonist or conversely praised for Lee's "universal" turn by writing about a character who might appear in a novel by John Updike. Both of these contradictory perspectives stem from the assumption that Lee was no longer writing "about race"—thus something to be dismissed by one camp and to be applauded in another. In the *New York Times Book Review,* A. O. Scott praised the novel's avoidance of "obsolete ethnic tribalism" in favor of "the deeper social concerns."[1] In perhaps the most condescending review, Lorna Bradbury, writing in the *Telegraph,* first projected that Lee was trying to transcend "mere" ethnic writing and then mockingly suggested his failure: "In his determination to move beyond the experience of a Korean immigrant, Lee appears, almost self-consciously, to be attempting his own Big American Novel in the vein of Richard Ford or Jonathan Franzen. . . . I ask whether he now sees himself as a Korean or an American writer. He replies that he is an 'American novelist,' but that this includes being a 'Korean writer.' 'In fact, sometimes, I think being a Korean-American novelist doesn't quite include being an American novelist, which is frustrating. . . .' He laughs, perhaps realizing how self-absorbed he sounds. This man of the suburbs can't seem to shake his Korean past."[2] The obsessive desire on the part of critics to categorize Lee's works in relationship to his race and ethnic identity led to reviews reflecting the critical anxiety caused by texts that do not easily fit into the categories expected of books marked—and marketed—as ethnic fiction.

Lee's lightly comic domestic drama in *Aloft* would seem a dramatic departure from the harrowing story in *A Gesture Life.* Self-referentially Lee has Jerry reflect on "deadly serious novels full of nourishing grace and humanity" that, despite their stories of purity and righteous conviction, are "about as satisfying as a radish" (*Aloft* 138). Instead, Jerry prefers to follow media coverage of the lost balloonist Sir Harold Eckes, "whose public trials are patent and palpable and, as in the worst of our own ideals, ultimately self-inflicted" (138). Unlike Lee's previous "serious" novels, *Aloft* seems to embrace absurdist comedy at times, but like his earlier works, it follows a protagonist who must come to grips with his own "self-inflicted" failings.

Lee's first three novels reveal their continuity in their narrators. Jerry Battle shares significant characteristics with Doc Hata. Both narrators are unreliable middle-aged men living emotionally detached lives in the suburbs of New York. In the critical concern over Jerry's race, the similarity in gender construction in the novels is overlooked. Jerry's white Italian American masculinity does not read very differently from that of the Korean American narrators in Lee's earlier novels. Lee's male narrators are all emotionally evasive and disconnected from those to whom they should be closest. All three are particularly inept in truly seeing women outside of their relationships to men.

While *Aloft* shares a preoccupation with masculine identity, Jerry's sense of national and racial identity is far more assured than that consideration is in either Doc Hata or Henry Park. Jerry is bold, assured of his role in society in an unself-conscious way that asserts his white privilege more than anything else in the novel. In fact, Jerry Battle is drawn as if Lee took the confidence and arrogance of Lelia's father in *Native Speaker* and made a more sympathetic portrait of him. What makes the novel so dynamic is the reader's push-pull of finding Jerry Battle charming while realizing his faults. *Aloft* is as much concerned with racial construction in the United States as Lee's earlier works are because Jerry Battle's perspective on the world is shaped by his complacent position as a white man. From his disconnected relationship with his Korean wife to his struggles to reconnect to his children, Battle must contend with his own emotional detachment and sense of entitlement in order to heal his family life. Lee's project in *Aloft* is to imagine the gradual evolution of white privilege through the figure of Jerry, the white, quietly racist grandfather who is painfully reeducated for the new, multicultural world.

The critic Mark C. Jerng attributed these mixed responses to Lee's novel to the book's being "what Shelley Fisher Fishkin calls a 'transgressive text' in which a writer of one race or ethnicity creates a main protagonist of another race or ethnicity."[3] From this analysis Jerng used *Aloft* as an example of how critics read Asian American literature with a predetermined set of expectations for what "ethnic literature" should be and said that reviewers were thus "contextualizing it with recognizable parameters of ethnic representation."[4] Jerng also analyzed how critics dealt with Lee's "disruptive" text either by conflating Jerry's Italian heritage with the Asian-descended characters of Lee's earlier works or by treating Jerry as a representation of universal experiences.[5] Although *Aloft* could be read "as performing a phenomenology of uneasy whiteness," Jerng warned that this reading could potentially lead back to reducing the narrator to "the universal subject surrounded by ethnic others."[6] Instead, Jerng stressed that careful recognition of how Jerry *perceives* race from his specific subject position highlights "these forms of perception instead of representations of whiteness [and] enables an analysis of the varied modes of perceiving race within the novel."[7] This distinction between a mere representation of whiteness and the position of Jerry's perspective reminds readers to analyze Jerry's narration with critical distance.

Building from Jerng's work, the critic Stephen Hong Sohn labeled the racial difference between author and narrator "racial asymmetry": "By positioning Jerry as the storyteller, the novel refracts the Asian American experience through the lens of a white character rather than presenting it, presumably more directly, through a figure assumed to be a fictionalized double for the author. A second level of racial asymmetry emerges as the novel exposes the blind spots in liberal individualist thinking; that is, Jerry conceives of his suburban life through a specific set of norms and regulations that place whiteness at the center and racial minorities as deviant bodies on the periphery. In such ways, *Aloft* dynamically spotlights narrative perspective and mode to erase a clear definition of racial authorial authenticity, to show how issues of race and identity unfold in specific formal and contextual registers."[8] The "racial asymmetry" that Sohn has identified in *Aloft* works to disrupt earlier views of Lee's novels as well. In this novel Lee implicitly resists the earlier critical analyses of his novels that tried to overlay biographical readings to his fictional works; subsequently *Aloft* makes that type of reading much more difficult.

Despite the initial popular dismissal of Lee's "transgressive" work, a small but growing body of scholarly criticism has seen Lee's use of a white protagonist as representative of a new move toward a "post-ethnic literary space."[9] Florian Sedlmeier has seen Lee refusing to force his work to bear the weight of ethnic representation. In *Aloft,* Lee most clearly refuses to comply with ethnic categorization as an Asian American writer, a subject he addressed in an interview with Christine Zilka: "I, too, felt sometimes trapped inside that moniker, but there are so many new Asian-American writers publishing today and I must think that the perception of who 'we' are is changing. We're writing all kinds of stories and in various modalities and styles, and it's getting more and more difficult to categorize us. Or at least for intelligent readers and critics to do so."[10] In another interview, titled "The Drama of Consciousness," Lee specifically addressed the subject position and perspective he imagined for his narrator in *Aloft:*

> There are plenty of stories about middle-aged angst and midlife crises with marital problems and what not. But this book isn't about aging. It's about someone who's been too comfortable in his life and is now trying to figure out what that all means. It's also in a way an immigrant story, but a couple of generations past. I was very interested in that. But I decided early on that the hero wouldn't be an Asian American character, because an Asian American character in that age in that setting would have required a very different story. It couldn't be a story about someone who felt like he completely fit and belonged in this context, or felt too comfortable. It just couldn't be. That's why it had to be someone who was white, but not so landed and established. I wanted someone who didn't question his belonging, and yet someone who still had ties to the old world.[11]

Here, Lee stressed the narrative possibilities that opened up to him when he made his narrator white: Jerry in *Aloft* writes from a position of unquestioned belonging. Because Lee was interested in examining a character who lives a largely unexamined life, he pointed to the seeming impossibility of an Asian American character experiencing such a feeling of absolute belonging. Jerry Battle, then, is a character defined by white privilege, here defined in part as the experience of feeling at complete ease within American culture. Even as he implies this interest in exploring the experience of white privilege in *Aloft,* Lee also carefully underscores the American commonality between Asian Americans and Italian Americans—the immigrant experience. What is revealed over the course of the novel, however, is how these racial differences lead to very different types of experiences.

That the narration is from the white, middle-aged, male subject position does not mean that race is not a significant preoccupation of the novel; in fact, Jerry's position in the world is such that race permeates the narration. Jerng noted that "all of Jerry's raced-based thoughts and perceptions occur in his commentary and none of them appear in his narrated dialogues with other persons. The novel exhibits a strict segregation of where race is: it is part of Jerry's long diatribes about life, but none of it occurs in the direct speech between him and others. In other words, race is everywhere in the novel but it is never talked about."[12] Jerry thinks in racial terms constantly but not without some self-consciousness, as his daughter, Theresa, is an academic who berates Jerry for his retrograde thinking. Jerry is the patriarch of a family he calls "a grab bag miscegenation," as Jerry's children are Italian from his side of the family and Korean from his now-deceased wife, Daisy's, side. While Jerry seems to think that his "mixed" family counters any residual racial judgments that creep into his head, the novel subtly undermines Jerry's confident convictions. In pondering the racial makeup of his family, Jerry thinks,

> As a group you can't really tell what the hell we are, though more and more these days the very question is apparently dubious, if not downright crass, at least to folks like Theresa and Paul, whose race-consciousness is clearly quite different from mine. I suppose what's critical to them is who's asking the question, for if it's an average white guy like me there's only awkwardness and embarrassment ahead, the assumption being that I'm going to blindly buy into a whole raft of historical "typologies" and "antecedents" and turn around and plonk somebody with the label of Other. This, by the way, is and isn't a terrible thing. They inordinately fear and respect the power of the word, having steadily drawn down distinctions between Life and Text. Let me say that when I was growing up the issues could be a lot heavier than that, a switchblade or Louisville Slugger being the *text* of choice, and one not so easily parsed or critiqued. (72–73)

The contrast of Jerry's "real world" perspective with Paul and Theresa's academic race consciousness shows how persuasive and charming Jerry's narration can be. At first glance the joke seems to be on these ridiculous academics whose conflicts have no physical stakes to rival those of the streets on which Jerry grew up. But Jerry's blindness to the significance of race and language is highlighted when this speech is followed by his suspicions that his son Jack has probably "passed" for white most of his life: "Jack, on the other hand, seems totally unconcerned about such matters, and always has been, but I can't say for certain, because we've never discussed the subject" (73). Jerry's dismissal of the significance of race in the real world is undermined by the psychological violence of racism on his children. This attitude is an example of what Sohn has called the "inferential racism at play within the novel, a form of subtle prejudice made explicit through Lee's use of refracted narration."[13] As a white man, Jerry has not had to confront racism in the same way that his children have. His conspicuous silence on the subject reveals how his position of privilege prevents a deeper connection to his son; his fears of being dismissed as "blindly buying" into racist thinking leads to passive parenting that contributes to Jack's insecurity.

Because of Jerry Battle's narrow consciousness, it is tempting to lump *Aloft* with the spate of American suburban novels appearing regularly since World War II. Lee's suburban Long Island setting, in particular, makes comparison to

John Cheever's short fiction and novels inevitable. Michiko Kakutani's review in the *New York Times,* prominently blurbed on the back cover of the paperback edition, compared the novel to work by John Updike, Walker Percy, and Cheever, thus situating the novel in an established literary tradition, albeit one beginning generations before Lee. Yet Lee's subtle alterations to the familiar themes of suburban literature in part update the genre. By reflecting the changing demographics of suburban life,[14] the critic Keith Wilhite has argued, "The novel takes the traditional postwar critique of suburban banality, alienation, and homogeneity and turns it on its head, not through a pastoralized fiction of the 1950s but by reconstructing that older model to make room for an ethnically diverse, non-nuclear family and the reality of economic hardship."[15] In sharp contrast to his view of works such as Jonathan Franzen's *The Corrections,* a novel that presents suburban living as "a counterfeit, fictitious way of life,"[16] Wilhite has seen the multiracial discourse of *Aloft* as part of a suburban recovery project, one that brings a more complex understanding of what suburban life means by using race "to unsettle our assumptions about suburban insularity."[17] *Aloft,* he posited, presents the oft-dismissed suburbs as a place far more cosmopolitan than previous versions of suburbia would suggest.

The quintessential denizen of Lee's suburbia is Jerry's son, Jack. Having taken over the family landscaping business so that Jerry could take an early retirement, Jack expands Battle Brothers beyond sustainability in a quest for growth to fund Jack's need to acquire more material signifiers of wealth and success. Living in a gated community in a "McMansion" (10) that is "more than three times bigger than the house he grew up in," Jack and his wife, Eunice, spare no expense in building and furnishing their home, including a Jay Gatsby–like library full of unread books (69). Expenses such as their master bedroom kitchenette cause Jerry to reflect that "this is the kind of lifestyle detail that brought down the railroad barons and junk bond kings and dotcommers and whoever else will next rocket up and flame out in misery" (93). Even though *Aloft* was published years before the U.S. housing bubble burst that led to a global recession, Jerry seems pointedly prescient in this treatment of Jack's unfettered greed. Like that of the railroad barons, this lifestyle is fueled by the labor of people of color both at home and at Battle Brothers. Jack's quick business growth causes him "to hire extra help literally off the street each morning in Farmingville, where the Hispanic men hang out" (25), while Eunice is dependent on her housekeeper Rosario, who in order to do the domestic work of keeping up the house and appearances, "stays six nights a week, only leaving on Sunday morning to spend a day and night with her husband and two children and mother, who live somewhere deep in Queens" (69).

The privilege of Jack and Eunice's nouveau riche status comes at the exploitation of working-class people of color.

Rather than simply condemn the excesses of Jack's lifestyle, Lee generously provides a portrait of what motivates Jack's excessive need for more. Jack Battle embodies many of the central concerns of the novel: racial, economic, and masculine insecurity. Jack's sense of inferiority appears to be embedded in his complicated relationships with his parents. Jack was a child when his mother, Daisy, drowned in the backyard swimming pool, and Jerry attributes Jack's excessive interest in achieving the appearance of success to his desire to "recast our family into one that might appear in a fashion magazine spread titled something like 'The Spoils of Battle'" (72). Although Jerry recognizes his son's need to compensate, he never sustains a deep sense of guilt for Jack's feelings of insecurity even when he directly implicates himself in that insecurity. In fact, Jerry suspects that Jack took over Battle Brothers in order to please him even though he did not care about his business legacy. Furthermore, Jerry acknowledges being gratified that Jack took control of the company so that he could shirk his responsibility to carry on his own father's work, "thereby committing the sin of tendering one generation's dreams for the illusory expectations of another, which is no doubt a practice wretched, and shameful, if time-honored" (296).

Knowing that his own selfish reasons are partly at work in Jack's business decisions, Jerry does not discuss the business with Jack after he is made aware of Jack's increasing levels of debt. It is Jerry's elderly father, Hank, who sees that Battle Brothers is failing, that Jack is in trouble, and that Jerry needs to intervene actively before his son self-destructs. As in *Native Speaker* when Henry's father and son are able to bridge the generation gap in a way that Henry cannot achieve, Jack is closer to Hank than Jerry is to either his father or his son. Against his father's wishes, Jerry puts Hank in Ivy Acres, a place that Hank calls an "air-conditioned corporate concentration camp" (181), and even Jerry admits that Ivy Acres spends much money keeping up the illusion of comfort for the benefit of the residents' children, who use its beauty to assuage their guilt in leaving their parents in a nursing home. Despite his own actions and his own admittedly distant relationships, Jerry secretly hopes for "the Invitation" from Jack and his wife to move in with them when he is too old to live alone. After suffering a heart attack and a stroke near the end of the novel, Hank does receive this invitation, and Jerry is honest enough to admit to himself that he is unlikely to receive the same consideration because "unlike Pop I'll probably be pushing hard for special treatment, and thus receive none in return" (327).

The communication that Hank advocates between his son and his grandson is impossible for Jerry, who has been taught a passive, silent form of masculine parenting from Hank. Hank, growing up Italian in the city amid racial strife and poverty, changed the family name from Battaglia to Battle and moved his father's bricklaying business to the suburbs. But this upward mobility did not protect them from loss, and when Jerry's older brother Bobby died in the Vietnam War, father and son were as silent about their grief as they were about Hank's frequent affairs. Men, Jerry learned early on, do not talk about their emotions. In her excellent article "The Business of Forgetting: Postwar Living Memorials and the Post-Traumatic Suburb in Chang-rae Lee's *Aloft,*" Kathy Knapp wrote, "Lee is not interested in tracing an inheritance of loss or the heavy burden of guilt as it moves from one beleaguered everyman to the next. In *Aloft,* the transgenerational phantom is no free-floating force that overtakes its victims. Instead, it is a carefully preserved legacy of complicity, defining not just the Battle family dynamics but [also] its long-successful business model: each principal of Battle Bros. Inc. has learned at his father's knee how to profitably cultivate a landscape designed to promote numbing forgetfulness."[18] Knapp viewed the family business as an economic practice that replicates the emotional detachment and evasion that characterize how the Battle men engage with the world. This business has been successful for decades as each succeeding American generation has tried to present a beautiful facade, but the failure of this model as a way to live is evident in Jack's financial collapse. Emotional avoidance, manifesting itself in excessive consumption that masks painful reality, is doomed to failure.

Jerry's hobby of flying is Lee's organizing metaphor for this character's emotional distance. The title of the novel, of course, refers to Jerry's state while flying and his desire to stay above emotional entanglement. Flying is peaceful for Jerry because "from up here . . . I can't see the messy rest, none of the pedestrian, sea-level flotsam that surely blemishes our good scene" (3). Shortly after his girlfriend Rita has left him, Jerry buys the plane from an interracial couple who have lost their son to a car accident. Shari attributes their previous inability to sell the plane to fears that the plane has "bad luck," but Hal thinks that potential buyers do not want a black man's plane. After Jerry makes it clear that he is still interested in buying the plane, Hal opens up and tells Jerry his story. Overcome with grief at the loss of his son Donnie, who was studying to become a doctor, Hal used the saved-up tuition money to buy a plane that he named in his son's honor, only to have a stroke midair. Although moved by the tragedy of the story, Jerry is uncomfortable with the emotion expressed by the couple and secretly wishes to "decline" the intimacy (18). Undeterred by the failure of Hal's efforts to fly above his trauma, Jerry uses the plane to avoid his realities on the ground.

Knapp argued that the novel can be read as a post-9/11 trauma narrative. Noting how quickly "the government sought to return the nation to a pre-9/11 status quo" in the wake of the attacks, she saw the novel as representing not "the conditions of large-scale catastrophe but instead those of an anxious, uncertain everyday in order to imagine a moral framework for bearing witness and responsibility in trauma's ongoing wake."[19] Knapp's argument reveals how central the events of 9/11 are to *Aloft* despite its seemingly conspicuous absence from direct treatment. The novel opens with Jerry flying alone in his Skyhawk over Long Island, a vantage point from which "everything looks perfect to me" (1). On this solo journey, he can "check the skyline for where the Twin Towers used to be" (21). This brief mention reminds the reader of the *absence* of the buildings and the trauma that rocked the nation; yet this reference is buried in the middle of a long sentence detailing Jerry's many travels around the area near his home. Jerry's narration is as evasive and misleading as his stunted emotional life is as he tries desperately to integrate the trauma of 9/11 into the everyday description.

The gaping hole of the Twin Towers is part of normal life now, mentioned but quickly passed over, with Jerry flying above it. In an interview Lee described how 9/11 influenced the novel he was working on at that time: "September 11 happened . . . and I just stopped writing. . . . I had faith in the idea that people would want to move on, and I thought, if there's anyone who wouldn't be dealing with such a thing it would be Jerry Battle."[20] In the interview Lee spelled out how Jerry's underreaction to 9/11 reveals his character. Since the novel is set on Long Island and was written in the aftermath of 9/11, it seems as though Jerry would be preoccupied by an event that shattered American illusions of impenetrability and security; Jerry is, after all, a man whose primary desires are comfort and lack of conflict. Instead we see Jerry respond with avoidance, a strategy of nonengagement.

According to Knapp, Jerry's emotional avoidance is what helps to revise the standard expectations for the suburban novel by exposing how Jerry's "insistent detachment" is predicated on his privilege.[21] Jerry's wife, Daisy, bears the brunt of her husband's emotional withdrawal. An immigrant from Korea whom Jerry meets while she is working in a department store, Daisy is remembered by Jerry after her death as an "old-fashioned girl in matters of family, not only because she wasn't so long removed from the old country, but also because of her nature (if you can speak of someone's nature, before she changed and went a little crazy and ended up another person entirely)" (107). Sohn suggested that Jerry's "liberal individualist thinking positions Daisy as a singular anomaly, a woman surprisingly gone mad, rather than as an immigrant facing a significant adaptive challenge due to a racially segregated setting."[22] Although Jerry praises Daisy for being an ideal housewife because of both her domestic capability and her sexual appeal, Jerry—and the reader—never truly knows who Daisy is. As Kristen Case stated in her review of the novel, "If Jerry cannot see Daisy as a person, neither can we. Lee offers no counterpoint to Jerry's version of Daisy, but allows us to feel its suffocating limitations, Jerry's terrible and ordinary failure."[23]

When Daisy starts showing signs of mental illness by breaking the expected gender roles in their marriage (the first signs being a less than spotlessly clean house and escalating to nude nighttime walks in the neighborhood), Jerry does not have the skills to cope. Admitting that "talk was never that important to us anyway," as Daisy's English was "just rudimentary enough for us to stay clear of in-depth and nuanced discussions, which suited me fine," Jerry cannot possibly begin to help his wife. Worse still, he has cut off her ability to speak with her family in Korea by forbidding the expensive long distance phone calls. Knapp has drawn a connection between Jerry's refusal to know his wife's past and the insistence by the dominant culture to forget immigrants' real identities: "While Daisy's being haunted by trauma is evident, the novel itself fully suppresses the details of Daisy's traumatic past: whatever haunts her remains unspoken. This conspicuous silence raises the moral stakes of Lee's decision to lend his narrative voice to a white middle-class male. . . . Jerry's wooing of Daisy and his subsequent efforts to separate her from a disturbing past he'd rather know nothing about mimics [*sic*] the assimilation process itself; their unhappy union illustrates how nullifying this process can be."[24] Although she initially seems to have assimilated to the role of ideal American housewife, Daisy, like Ahjuma in *Native Speaker,* remains the unknowable Korean immigrant woman. Like Henry Park, Jerry Battle sees only the comfortable results of female labor, not the real woman performing it.

Jerry's relationship with his wife is similar to his father's relationship with Jerry's mother. At a young age, Jerry learns to disrespect women. His father so patently disregards his wife that he brings his son along when he is unfaithful to Jerry's mother, poisoning Jerry's parental relationships and establishing Jerry's sense of what women are worth. Jerry's later reflections on his mother's life, however, are more generous than his youthful ones: "My mother, God bless her soul, was nothing if not dependable. It's a terrible thing to admit, but I used to think she wasn't the swiftest doe in the forest, because she rarely did anything else but keep house and feed everybody and try to make Pop's life run smoothly and comfortably, even as he was often a jerk to her and had several love affairs and was universally acknowledged to be a Hall of Fame Jerk. . . . Lately I've been thinking that her lack was more emotional than intellectual; it wasn't because the gray matter didn't work well enough but that she preferred to keep her life as uncomplicated as possible, more thought and rumination leading only to misery and remorse and the realization that she could never leave him, that she could never really start over" (120–21). This recognition reveals Jerry to be a product of both of his parents; his childish demands to be catered to by the women in his life come from his father, but his emotional avoidance comes from his beleaguered mother.

His parents' marriage provides a poor model for Jerry in his own marriage. When Daisy charges a third of Jerry's annual salary at Bloomingdale's during a manic episode, Jerry disengages from the family and, on the advice of his father, treats Daisy poorly to help her learn her place. Of course, neither of these strategies works, and Daisy's depression worsens. After she lunges at Jerry with a knife, he takes her to the family doctor, a man not qualified to treat mental illness. This turns out to be a mistake, as the doctor prescribes a depressant that may have contributed to Daisy's death by possible suicidal drowning. Jerry admits that he was thinking only of "needing to jam hard on the brakes, do whatever it took to stop the train" (129). Daisy's illness is exacerbated by her husband's inability to connect emotionally.

After her death, Jerry's denial continues and harms the children in ways he does not even years later fully understand. Although Jack is a gifted swimmer, Jerry immediately fills in the pool in which Daisy died, and he marvels at Jack's quick recovery as Jack throws himself into other sports, even attributing some of this "recovery" to his own actions: "Maybe the key to returning to normalcy was my quick response, my instant renewal of our little landscape, that I filled in and bulldozed over the offending site and rolled out perfect new sod that they could at least play upon without a care or thought, if never really frolic in the same way again" (241). Jerry literally fills up the hole of his wife's death with sod in hopes of a fresh start. Jack, of course, is not recovered, but he has learned from his father how to keep emotions hidden. Worse still, we learn at the end of the novel that Jerry has never placed a tombstone on Daisy's grave; he has left her grave literally unmarked for decades. Daisy is all but erased from the family under the force of Jerry's denial.

Jerry becomes even more dedicated to evading emotional responsibility. He begins a more than twenty-year relationship with Rita, a Puerto Rican woman he initially hires to cook, clean, and care for his children. Initially appealing for her cooking, Rita packs up her expensive cookware when she leaves Jerry in full knowledge that "this would pain" him (47). Although he lived with Rita and let her raise his children, Jerry never married her, reassuring himself that "I'd thought I was treating her like a queen" (63). Like Daisy, Rita is a woman of color working in a service position when Jerry meets her, and also like Daisy, she is a source of food, comfort, and sex. In one scene he compares their bodies to the "too thin and sharply featured" white, professional women he meets at the tennis court: "Daisy was slim, but she had a round moon face and was unusually supple of body, and Rita, of course, is a lovely plenteous armful, legful, everything else, which I'm sure makes a man like me not really yearn to conquer or destroy or run my part of the world, but rather just dwell and loll and hope to float a little, relinquish the burdens" (195).

While ostensibly resisting the image of white, conquering male, this passage reinforces the racial and class dynamics at work in Jerry's preference in partners. The only "battle" Jerry Battle ever fights is to accept the challenge of a tennis match against Rita's new boyfriend, Richie Coniglio. Although out of shape and out of practice, Jerry beats Richie at tennis to "make Richie pay for what we both should have done" (207). While the match is really all a result of male ego and competition, Rita breaks off her relationship with Richie and begins to see Jerry again as a result of this ambivalent display of love.[25]

Jerry's escapist mind-set is reinforced again by his job as a part-time travel agent after he retires from Battle Brothers at the earliest opportunity. Theresa calls him "the last living white man" and calls his travels "rapacious, hegemonic colonialist 'projects'" (29). While working at the travel agency, Jerry befriends Miles Quintana, a Dominican teenager hired to diversify the office. Miles does not actually speak Spanish fluently, but he still helps bring in Latino business, "proving it's not always the linguistical intricacies that people find reassuring, but broader, deeper forms of communication" (36). While Jerry finds it amusing that Miles was hired for his assumed ability to speak Spanish, he does recognize that Miles's presence in the office communicates a sense of belonging to the Latino community that the agency was targeting. Even as he admires Miles's ability to communicate through more than language, Jerry recognizes himself as "a person who is taken much more by what people say than by what they do. I tend to overrecognize signifiers, to quote my daughter; I'm easily awestruck by symbol and tone" (37).[26] Jerry fails to understand how and what the people in his life are really communicating to him. His refusal to see beyond surface performances makes him an extremely unreliable narrator, and Lee reminds his readers throughout the novel not to read Jerry's thoughts as literal truth.

It is Jerry's self-professed difficulty with human interpretation that makes his bond with his son-in-law, Paul Pyun, that much more unexpected. Paul is a "somewhat famous" writer who has written three novels and "can put together a nice-sounding sentence or two and does it with feeling but never quite gets to the point" (78). Jerry describes Paul's subject matter as "The Problem with

Being Sort of Himself—namely, the terribly conflicted and complicated state of being Asian and American and thoughtful and male, which would be just dandy in a slightly different culture or society but in this one isn't the hottest ticket" (78). Here, Lee teases the reader with a Rothian move, daring us not to conflate the author with his character.[27] Paul's sensitivity and skill with language and analysis seem antithetical to Jerry's clumsy path through life.

The commonality between Jerry and Paul becomes clearer when Theresa announces that she has life-threatening cancer but is delaying treatment until after her pregnancy. Even though her husband and her father do not agree with her choice, both men stay silent on the subject. Reminiscent of Lee's personal essays, particularly "Coming Home Again," about cooking for his family while his mother was dying of stomach cancer, Paul sublimates his emotions by cooking elaborate, time-consuming meals.[28] While the food, of course, pleases Jerry, he begins to wish that Paul would break down, as "all the goddamn Eastern restraint . . . is, of late, becoming a kind of torture to me" (216). Although Jerry attributes Paul's silence to his race, Jerry takes no steps to intervene. Like his father-in-law, Paul is not talking to Theresa "in any way that counts" (218). Language mastery alone does not equal true communication.

Tellingly, Jerry's most honest and intimate conversation occurs moments before Theresa's death. While flying with Theresa on a day trip, he learns from her that Jack had recently told her he had been at home just before Daisy's death. This new information about Jack's story reminds Jerry that clearly Daisy had not been drinking alone that afternoon, a fact he had suppressed. Jack's observation that Daisy's pool floats had been taken out of the pool before his mother drowned also indicates more clearly that Daisy's death was a suicide. Decades after Daisy's death, Jerry is only now able to piece together a full picture of his wife's last day through secondhand information that should have come directly from his son. Theresa pushes Jerry further by expressing her anger that he did not allow the children time to grieve. Jerry's emotional disturbance is mirrored by actual air turbulence, and he struggles to control the plane as they lose "1000 feet, an entire skyscraper" (344), reminding us of the fall of the Twin Towers. Jerry manages to steady the plane, but in a scene reminiscent of the story of the original owner's stroke midair, Theresa hemorrhages, and Jerry struggles to land the plane as quickly as possible. He wonders if this is "the moment of payback for my years of exclusively fair-weather flying" (347). As Jerry finally confronts his past, this scene makes clear how his children have suffered the repercussions of his emotional distance and racial privilege.

The scene of Theresa's death brings the novel full circle, back to its beginnings and the story of how Jerry's plane got its name. Even though Jerry is able to understand racism only secondhand in his encounter with Hal and Shari, he does learn the pain of a child's death firsthand when he too suddenly loses his multiracial child who had been facing a bright future. Jerry's whiteness does not make him immune to the pain of life. In looking for a way to get high above the "mess" of living, he is brought low by the curse of the plane.

While the implication is clear at the end of chapter 11, Theresa's death is not directly narrated or mentioned in Jerry's narration of chapter 12. The novel's organization frequently mimics Jerry's evasive narration by switching focus at each new chapter. After the catastrophe in the air, the final chapter begins with Jerry fully grounded and with new responsibilities. Theresa's son, named Barthes Tae-Jon Battle in honor of the French literary critic Roland Barthes, is born premature but growing.[29] In a sentiment similar to Lelia Park's in *Native Speaker* after the birth of her son, Jerry thinks that "the only thing that makes me pause for a half second is not that he doesn't look anything like me, which is how it has to be, but that I can't quite see his mother in him either, not yet, anyway, as he is an exact replica of the infant Paul's parents have shown us in pictures from his baby album" (354). While it would be easy to present this moment as yet another example of Jerry's racial preoccupation, his interest here seems to be one of mourning; he is looking for his lost daughter in her child. This moment echoes Lelia's concern that Mitt does not resemble her in *Native Speaker.* In addition, like Mitt, this baby bears the symbolic weight of the multiracial child who embodies hopes for the future. Knapp noted that "the violent birth of a mixed-race child enables the transformative power of the collective memory of loss to redefine the contours of community."[30] Unable to deny the loss of Theresa, Jerry must reconfigure his life.

Acting on advice from Theresa shortly before her death, Jerry invites Jack and his family to move into his house. In a reversal of Jerry's hoped-for "Invitation," all of the remaining Battles are living in Jerry's modest suburban home at the end of the novel. After Jack loses the family business and confesses the state of their finances to his wife, Eunice has a comic emotional breakdown at the Saks counter and destroys her credit cards. This most openly status-conscious member of the family, however, adjusts to her reduced circumstances because she is, as Jerry narrates, "genuinely devoted to Jack, duly remaking her bed minus all the silk shams and throws" (555). Jack and Eunice's marriage is actually strengthened by the collapse of their lifestyle. Jerry is happy to have his family living together in the family house, but he also imagines a future time when he and Rita move to their own "closing digs" (356). Jerry is not completely changed from his earlier self, but as Knapp has argued, "It is the persistence of loss that stands as the foundation for meaningful connection with others": "the novel's insistent uncertainty undercuts the neoliberal values that have come to be synonymous with suburbs—individual mastery, security, the 'good life'—and suggests new possibilities for being and belonging in an indeterminate aftermath."[31]

The novel concludes with Jerry climbing into a hole that Jack has dug in the backyard to put in a pool. Jerry, whom the reader first meets flying above the earth, now lies deep in the earth: "Unlined as yet with concrete and tiles, it's a huge dark shoebox, the earth cool and still moist in the corners and along the deep end. And as scary and unnervingly quiet as it is to be even this far below ground, I do like the smell, which is loamy and fat and sweetly vernal, not at all of extinction, and I breathe in as deeply as I can bear. I've found myself coming down here once or twice a day, standing and sitting and then leaning back against the steeply ramped dirt, gazing up at a perfect frame of firmament for flights endless, unseen" (364). Through this "excavation" of the site of his wife's death, Jerry is simultaneously confronting his past and contemplating his future (364). Evasive, distant Jerry is now in a sort of daily therapy, confronting reality "as deeply" as he can. Knapp viewed the ending as reflecting the need to interrogate both personal and historical traumas: "The novel may begin with Jerry at a safe remove as he soars over the Twin Towers' open grave, but its final image leaves him fully immersed in a crater of his own making, suggesting that the premise of upward mobility is not just an implausible fiction, but a cruel story in dire need of revision."[32] Jerry may have been "safe" at the beginning of the novel, but only at the conclusion, when he is mired in the past, is he truly able to connect to the present.

Wilhite read the conclusion of the novel as a significant reclamation of the possibilities of the suburban narrative: "*Aloft* works through the familiar, aerial shots of uniform suburbs and brings us to the ground, where the perspective gets more complicated. The reconstruction projects taking place around Jerry invert the impulse toward insularity, and though it is just one 1950s-era house, the multifamily Battle home invites readers to complete a recalibrated scale of suburban living."[33] While the new iteration of the Battle home is indeed a space of "recalibrated" living, Jerry's ability to participate fully is still a work in progress. Being called into the house to join the others for lunch, Jerry does not immediately respond to "the barely audible sound traveling just above and far enough away" (364). Down in his hole, Jerry is near enough to his family to hear them, but he is not fully ready to join them. Yet, Jerry also recognizes now that he is not the center of the family, the center of the story: "It's okay. No problem. They'll start without me, you'll see" (364). Like *Native Speaker* and *A Gesture Life, Aloft* ends with an ambiguous sense of tentative possibility.

It is the family as a body, not Jerry as an individual, that ultimately matters most in this "recalibrated" world. Jerry may or may not be able to pull himself out of the hole of the past to be fully a part of his family. Near the end of the novel, Jerry recounts a story about his neighbor George Guggenheimer. When George's backyard koi pond causes a sinkhole in his yard that threatens to bankrupt him, he breaks down in front of Jerry in a manner that violates the suburban code of silence around debt. While politely comforting George, Jerry uncomfortably realizes that he has implied that he will help his neighbor; he is a landscaper, after all. Jerry, however, has no intention of loaning out Battle Bros. equipment or labor and knows that he will only "commiserate from a distance" (285). Before Jerry needs to extricate himself from the situation, George wins the lottery and all of his financial problems disappear. But new problems quickly take their place. George becomes overwhelmed with a fear of death and becomes an agoraphobe, and subsequently his wife divorces him and moves his children out of state. George gains money but loses his family and his connection to the outside world. The critique of class striving and desire for material goods at the expense of human relations that Lee begins in earnest in *A Gesture Life* is more fully developed in *Aloft* and becomes the focus of Lee's 2014 novel, *On Such a Full Sea*.[34] In these novels Lee suggests that the only counter to the traumas and alienation of modern living is the network of human connections to be built in a community, and Jerry Battle still has work to do.

CHAPTER 5

"Differing scales, unlikely modulations"

The Surrendered (2010)

In his first three novels, Chang-rae Lee uses unreliable first-person narration to illustrate the way the detached male characters engage and evade their true emotions. With his 2010 novel, *The Surrendered,* Lee broke with this perspective to write a historical war epic that spans from Japanese-occupied Manchuria in the 1930s, to Korea in the 1950s, to New York and Italy in the 1980s. The novel follows the intersecting lives of June, a Korean orphan; Hector, an American soldier; and Sylvie, the enigmatic missionary whom they both love. These characters meet in the aftermath of the Korean War in a newly established orphanage, and all are haunted by their past experiences. Lee envisioned the perspective shift "sort of as a mural": "[This] fit into the idea that these characters, in the scale of things, are very small. As people in wartime are. They have no real control over what happens to them. I saw these characters as little pieces of dust. Grains of sand, under this wheel of history. So I didn't want the 'I' to be so prominent in each of their cases."[1] Rather than focus on the singular, individual perspective of a Henry Park, a Doc Hata, or a Jerry Battle, Lee attempted a story that operates on a larger scale even as it focuses on the small everyday actions of three central characters. The novel operates much like June Han's theory of storytelling when selling antiques: "Authenticity ultimately lay in the story you could tell, a tale most effective when it was at once fanciful and mundane. You had to offer differing scales, unlikely modulations, though all based upon the firmest-seeming foundation" (*The Surrendered* 255). While it is undoubtedly his most ambitious work, this novel bears thematic and stylistic continuity with the earlier novels; although *The Surrendered* is Lee's first novel in the third person, it focuses as much on the inner turmoil of its multiple characters as on its sweeping plot.

Reception of *The Surrendered* was largely positive, and it was nominated for a Pulitzer Prize in 2011.[2] Many critics noted the similarity of the novel to Michael Ondaatje's 1992 novel *The English Patient,* an epic romantic love story that takes place at the end of World War II in Italy and recounts a love triangle that ends in the premature death of the beloved. In addition to this clear influence, Lee has claimed Ernest Hemingway's 1925 short story collection *In Our Time* as an inspiring model for capturing war experience, because "as you read [it], there's a dropping away of everything else."[3] As in Hemingway's writing, Lee's prose in many striking scenes in the novel only gestures to the emotional depths beneath the surface. Lee's elegant language is focused on revealing interiority provoking emotional reactions in his readers.

While Lee depicts Sylvie's confrontation with imperial Japanese forces in Manchuria and recounts both June's and Hector's firsthand experiences of the Korean War, much of the novel dwells on the psychological aftermath of these traumas. While the novel depicts two twentieth-century wars, *The Surrendered* was written during the U.S. wars in Iraq and Afghanistan. Reflecting on the American wars of the last decade while writing *The Surrendered,* Lee remarked in an interview that the novel is "really not just about the Korean War: it's about many conflicts, and I very consciously did that."[4] War permeates the novel despite the limited number of scenes that actually take place during wartime, putting the emphasis in the novel less on the particulars of these specific conflicts than on the ways people rebuild—or fail to rebuild—their lives after experiencing war. The puzzle of the title leads readers to ask questions: Who are the surrendered in the novel and what have they surrendered? Interestingly, the Korean title given to Lee's novel translates to "The Survivors."[5] *The Surrendered* is, of course, an ironic title for a book about a war that ended in an armistice with no official surrender on either side. However, "The Survivors" suggests a positive interpretation that the ambiguity of *The Surrendered* does not. Lee's title suggests defeat and vulnerability and provokes many of the central questions driving the novel: How does one live with the brutalities of his or her past? How much moral responsibility does one bear in the act of surviving? How much of one's life is the result of fate versus choice? The troubled lives of June, Hector, and Sylvie show the seemingly small but vastly significant differences between surviving and surrendering.

Lee began the novel more than a decade before publishing it. He started the book after completing *Native Speaker* but abandoned early attempts in order to focus on *A Gesture Life* and *Aloft.*[6] While this could be because *The Surrendered* is Lee's most formally ambitious work with a sprawling plot and multiple central characters, it is also in many ways his most autobiographically intimate novel. He dedicates the work to his sister, Eunei. One of the most poignant moments of the novel comes in the first chapter when a young June Han watches her younger brother die after a fall from the roof of an overpacked train of refugees. This scene was inspired by the true story of Lee's father's flight from North Korea during the war, when he, like June, saw his brother die after a fall that amputated his leg. His father lost a sister to pneumonia and his brother to a horrific accident, but these stories went untold until his son excavated this family history and imaginatively filled in the gaps. In an interview Lee recounted his inspiration for the wrenching opening chapter of *The Surrendered:* "That first journey of June's is an imagined version of a journey that my father took, where he was with his family around the eve of the war. In his story, he's just traveling with his family, and one night, he said, he lost his brother in a train accident. The more I got out of him, the more I realized it was what would become the train accident scene in the book. But that always struck me as remarkable—here was a man who was so composed, who would never express in any way, consciously or unconsciously, any blowback from those times. I was amazed—he lived through the war and never talked about it. That obviously was the spark for *The Surrendered*."[7] Even in this account of his father's experience in connection to the novel, Lee stressed not the horrors of the event but instead his father's reaction. It was how his father dealt with such a personal history that intrigued Lee as an author. In the same interview Lee said, "In his way, my father did his best not to exhibit any signs of what happened to him. The book is the opposite of that."[8] The central characters of *The Surrendered* are not successful in overcoming or concealing the repercussions of their traumatic life stories, and the frequent temporal shifts of each character's story line reinforce Lee's goal of showing the ways that past events never really leave people's presents and continue to shape their futures.

Although the first line of the novel promises the end of a journey, June's story of the loss of her family during the Korean War is the beginning point for Lee's exploration of the afterlife of war trauma. The novel begins in 1950 with June Han at age eleven caring for her younger twin siblings as they, with thousands of others, flee to the south of Korea during the civil war.[9] There the stories of the fates of June's family members are told. Members of the Republic of Korea (ROK) army murder her father, who is denounced as a Communist. Her brother is conscripted and sent to fight in the north. Her mother and sister resist sexual assault only to be killed by bombs. June takes responsibility for her younger siblings, and the extreme deprivations of their circumstances leave eleven-year-old June to contemplate the limits of human endurance: "She would give her life for them, but she had begun to understand that the other face of that will was that she could allow them to suffer only so much" (26). June's love for her siblings extends to contemplating poisoning them all to prevent their slow starvation. Although only a child herself, she, like Toni Morrison's Sethe, knows that there are fates worse than death and views mercy killing her family as an act of love.

June's steely resolve on this issue is not tested because fate intervenes when her siblings fall from the roof of a refugee train. Although her sister dies before June locates her, June finds her brother Ji-Young still alive but slowly dying. After realizing that she cannot carry him back to the train, she lays her brother down, and he asks her to promise to come back for him. Even though June agrees, Ji-Young releases her from this promise, and June leaves her brother behind to run for the train.

The psychological repercussions of this decision are evident in June's future relationships. The second chapter jumps forward to 1986 in New York City, where a recently widowed June is dying from stomach cancer and about to embark on a journey to Italy to reunite with her long-estranged son, Nicholas, before her death. Despite her seeming financial success, June's isolation, like that of Doc Hata in *A Gesture Life,* is readily apparent. Her last act before leaving the city where she has spent most of her adult life is to give furniture to her building's doorman, Habi. A Congolese refugee, Habi, like June, bears physical and psychological scars from civil war. They are not close friends, but June plans after her death to leave him a sum of money that is intentionally modest because "she didn't want him to have to think of her always in gratitude, which turns, too often, to resentment" (38). June's awareness of the debts and credits of human relationships seems particularly astute, if not heart-warming. But June's affection for Habi, the critic Stephanie Hsu noted, reveals a deeper connection: "June's and Habi's disfigurement in foreign conflict leads to affinity race cannot: This critique calls attention to the cultural and political injunction for disabled subjects to overcome the trauma of assimilation to the national body, which is imagined as a collective of able-bodied citizens, by hiding their impairments and disavowing bodily pain."[10] Hsu's provocative argument reveals Lee's use of disability in the novel to present the struggles of immigrants who must pass—as able-bodied and as American—in order to participate in American society, a performance that denies the brutality of their experience.[11]

Hsu's argument also highlights the circumstances of these immigrants' decisions to move to the United States: to escape violence caused by civil wars backed by foreign powers. In *Immigrant Acts: On Asian American Cultural Politics,* Lisa Lowe described the impetus of the surge in "new wave" Asian immigration: "Another distinguishing feature of the post-1965 Asian immigration is the predominance of immigrants from South Korea, the Philippines, South

Vietnam, and Cambodia, countries deeply affected by U.S. colonialism, war, and neocolonialism. Despite the usual assumption that Asians immigrate [*sic*] from stable, continuous, 'traditional' cultures, most of the post-1965 Asian immigrants come from societies already disrupted by colonialism and distorted by the upheavals of neocolonialism and war. The material legacy of the repressed history of U.S. imperialism in Asia is borne out in the 'return' of Asian immigrants to the imperial center."[12] While June leaves Korea before the loosening of immigration restrictions in 1965, Lowe's argument applied just as well to refugees from the Korean War; in fact, the plight of Korean orphans greatly contributed to the rewriting of U.S. immigration law. With Korea in turmoil after the end of the war and her family destroyed, June, a de facto colonial subject, "returns" to the United States just as Lowe suggested.

Lee directly associates June's war-time trials to her slow, agonizing death from cancer: "It was almost laughably ironic, that the cancer should be in her stomach. That she would die with her belly full. Hadn't she made that very pact a hundred times, a thousand times, when she was marching on the dismal road? Let me eat until I can't, let me fill this infinite cave, and I'll die right here. I'll surrender. And thus here she was, never to feel anything like hunger again. But she might take it on now, in trade for her life, that clenching weight of famishment" (58). More than thirty years after the hardships of the war, June is again bargaining for her survival. Undeniably facing imminent death, June is at first not ready to accept this fully. Her doctor recommends aggressive therapy and is so determined to refuse surrender that he does not hear June when she finally refuses to continue her treatments. The doctor's presenting an absolutist philosophy of treatment is at odds with June's own childhood acceptance that there should be limits to acceptable suffering. The doctor's arrogant and aggressive attitude is fundamentally American; June, however, has been taught through the Korean War a different philosophy, albeit one she resists. The vivid details and emotional complexity of the depiction of June's cancer painfully recall the details of the death of Lee's mother, Inja, in his autobiographical essays. Echoing Theresa's refusal of treatment in *Aloft* and previewing Lee's questioning of excessive cancer treatment in *On Such a Full Sea,* June's battle with the disease is his most developed critique of the diminished quality of life that cancer treatment brings and the rhetoric of warfare that American cancer discourse suggests. As she is a character whose entire life is devoted to survival, June's seeming "surrender" to cancer is not a moral defeat; it is her strength of will that allows her to end her medical care and die in a manner of her own choosing.

In a telling detail, June's bodily transformation caused by the cancerous tumor growing in her stomach reminds her of her pregnancy with her only child,

Nicholas: “She placed her hand on her stomach now and it was as if she felt him there instead of the huge dense egg of the tumor that had taken her over and spread itself in every part” (245). June’s relationship with her son begins in abjection, as he is conceived in desperation and her nausea during pregnancy is so extreme that she accepts that she may need an abortion. When Nicholas is born via caesarian section, June “actually gagged through her tears of wonderment . . . and the first words she said to him were, I’m sorry” (246). June’s motherhood begins and ends with apology. As a distant, ambivalent mother, “her focus on him alternated between being unrelentingly sharp and then dialed back so wide that the boy was but a ripple in the broad field of her vision, a mark of pale, this faint smudge of her blood” (247). In her lowest moments, June feels her son to be a burden and a liability: “He wasn’t deeply distressed—it was the softest crying, self-muffled, if that was possible—and although it would have been the simplest thing to wake and comfort him, she inexplicably stood over him in the dark, staring at his racked mouth and the tight, quivering shrug of his shoulders, and it took everything in her to renounce the thought that here was a boy she would have to carry about forever” (249). The brutality of June’s feelings here recalls the early scene in which she literally stops carrying her brother in order to save her own life. Unable and unwilling to abandon her child, June squelches the thought, but a lifetime of self-preservation makes her unable to relate to her son in a functional, healthy way.

Whereas Nicholas’s innocent, childlike weakness causes resentment in June, when she watches him steal from a store just for the pleasure of the act of theft, she is gratified, “for it was the picture of his surface equanimity, his self-mastery, that she was so gratified to see, to watch him exert himself upon the world, when the rest of the time he seemed to willingly subject to its turns” (252–53). Like the troubled Sunny in *A Gesture Life,* Nicholas has found small rebellions to be means of gaining a sense of power in a world shaped by a distant, yet controlling parent. Unsurprisingly, Nicholas leaves home at the first opportunity and has limited contact with his mother, communicating only through occasional phone calls and later postcards. June carries on with her life, but when she is awakened one night by a long distance phone call informing her that her son is in the hospital, she denies she has a son and hangs up the phone. She regrets this refusal immediately, but she is unable to establish contact with Nicholas and loses track of him. Close to death, June hires a private investigator named Clines to locate her son in Europe and begins her final journey to find Nicholas and seek his forgiveness.

Clines’s investigation leads June back to Hector Brennan, the man who delivered her to an orphanage at the end of the war, who later married her to bring her to the United States, and in an isolated encounter, unknowingly fathered

Nicholas. June finds Hector living in poverty and working as a janitor in Fort Lee, New Jersey. Living like a zombie, he considers "himself as among the creeping living dead" (100). Antithetical to June's tenacious self-preservation, Hector's lifestyle is an intentional form of self-effacement: "he knew his near-indigence was also easy cover, a way to hide and be freed from responsibility for anything in the least vital or important, which in effect was to be freed from the present, and the foreseeable future, if never quite the past" (97). Like many of the other characters in *The Surrendered,* Hector is consumed by his past, and he lives his life as a form of self-inflicted punishment for his sins.

Born in Ilion, New York, and named in honor of the Trojan warrior, the character Hector is heavily overlaid with symbolic import.[13] His loving but alcoholic father, Jackie Brennan, is a factory worker who quotes Thucydides and waxes philosophical at the bar (62). When asked why he named him Hector and not Achilles, Jackie replies, "Because a man wants a son for a son, and has no use for a champion" (62). His son points out that Hector dies and fails to protect his city and his family in the epic poem, but Jackie insists that Hector can change the story and that he can live forever. Hector is a loyal son whose weekly responsibility is to escort his father home safely after a night of drinking. One night, however, Hector leaves the bar early in order to have a tryst with a local woman whose husband is missing in action in World War II. Jackie's body is found a week later in the river. Hector's perception of his lack of filial loyalty, so unlike that of his namesake and yet with the same result, leads to his life of reckless, unheroic behavior. Named for an honorable but failed hero, Hector seeks death and thinks of himself as an antihero who curses those who come near him.

Despite his father's warning, Hector seeks out the Korean War, "not for the sake of fighting or killing anyone or defending his country, but for the selfish cause of punishing himself, and so proving his father right" (69). Like Homer's hero, he participates in a doomed war that he does not believe in. Despite his suicidal mission, Hector remains a moral soldier. When he witnesses two American soldiers blowing a trumpet into the ears of a young Chinese prisoner of war,[14] Hector saves the boy from further torture only to be ordered to kill the prisoner himself. When Hector is unable to do so, the prisoner is recaptured by his torturers until they finish with him and return him to Hector. When the prisoner pleads with Hector to kill him to end his suffering, Hector cannot bring himself to do it. Whereas June can contemplate the necessity of killing her beloved siblings to prevent their pain, Hector cannot kill this boy who has no chance of survival. He recognizes that it would be an act of mercy, but he cannot commit murder. The boy grabs a grenade from Hector's belt and kills himself.

Hector's punishment for his failure to cooperate with the men of his unit is his reassignment to the Graves Units, the group of black soldiers responsible for disposing of the bodies after battle. Although they joke that "every man is a black man in the end" as they clean up the rotted corpses, Hector's punishment—including his self-inflicted punishment—is characterized by racial "slumming." Years after the war, Hector settles in the Korean immigrant enclave of Fort Lee, New Jersey, a city described as "not long ago Jewish and Irish and Italian and now lighted around the clock like any street in Seoul or Shanghai with its flashing neon scripts and ideograms" (88). While Hector's lack of racial prejudice is unexpected for a working-class man of his era, the motivation behind this interaction is more about a desire to punish himself than any high-minded idealism. Even though Hector is a man so handsome as to have been a literal poster boy for World War II propaganda, he intentionally sabotages his privileges as a white man as part of his commitment to self-debasement.

That Hector's poverty is a result of personal choice is further reinforced by several gestures toward alternative lives that Hector might have lived if the war had not happened. In one such example, Hector is presented as a middle-class family man who "would simply have worked at Remington, if not in arms, then in typewriters, adding machines, whatever else" (103). This vision of a happy, suburban alternative Hector seems to fulfill the apple-pie wholesomeness of his poster-boy image: Hector Brennan, living the American dream. But the small detail of working for Remington, maker of arms and consumer goods, deflates the fantasy of the American good life by linking it to the warfare and death that feed the U.S. economy and allow for the postwar boom of prosperity. Hector, for all his poverty, alcoholism, and emotionally disconnected life, is outside the dominant system of exploitation that undergirds American wealth. In this marginalized status, he is more closely allied to his disenfranchised neighbors. The difference, of course, is that Hector has chosen his exile.

Despite his intentional isolation, Hector has embarked on a fragile relationship with another alcoholic, Dora. When she visits his apartment for the first time, Hector reflects on the state of his life: "No one had ever visited before, and he wouldn't have cared anyway, but mostly the apartment was messy because he no longer registered the layers of grime and dust. For if you suspected you were immortal, if you were afraid you might never be extinguished, the evidence of which had accrued enough over the years to convince him to almost believe its truth—the way his wounds, even the seemingly grave ones he'd suffered during the war, healed with magical swiftness; that he had aged in a way that appeared to the eye as if there were no other time except this one, no prior or future state—the concern for something like cleanliness, strangely enough, receded" (288–89). Hector's seemingly ageless, untouched body confirms for him his father's belief in his own immortality. This immortality, of course, is more appropriately associated with Achilles, the demigod immune to mortal wounds save his one secret weakness. Yet in *The Iliad,* Hector's body too remains unmarked; when Achilles tries to desecrate Hector's body after killing him, the gods protect Hector's body from harm. By applying this reading, Hector Brennan is not immortal; in fact, he is already dead, frozen in time.

When Dora threatens to bring Hector back to the present, Hector feels "a rent in his chain-mail vest" (284); he begins to see the possibility of a happier future. This is when June reenters his life. In a sudden plot twist, June's private detective accidentally kills Dora in a car accident, which again leads Hector to believe he is cursed. Yet it is in this cursed state that Hector feels most comfortable: "His heart felt smashed every time he pictured Dora, but if he was honest it soon revived with what he had to believe was a rush of liberty, if liberty degraded, this feeling that he was released once again from the onus of having to hope or dream" (351).

Hector's "curse" keeps him tied to June Han. Although they were once married and have a son, what truly unites Hector and June is their shared experience after the end of the Korean War at an orphanage called New Hope. There they both fell in love with Sylvie Tanner, the wife of the Christian missionary who ran the orphanage. Hector and June were drawn to Sylvie, perhaps because she was a deeply troubled woman. The daughter of aid workers for the Red Cross, Sylvie Binet traveled the world with her parents but felt insignificant in comparison to their commitments to social justice. She felt "shame at her own selfishness and self-pity seemed monstrously childish in the face of her parents' unstinting efforts" (182): "They were people who took seriously every action and effort, brooking high risks if necessary, for it was all in the service of what they saw as the most urgent calling in this life: educating children, feeding the poor, ameliorating suffering. Throughout her childhood they traveled from destitute place to destitute place, from the Amazon to West Africa and then to Asia, and although she always felt their love for her, she could feel cast apart from them as well, set just outside the tight centripetal force of their labors, the impassioned orbit of their work" (181).

With the Binets, Lee begins an exploration of the nature of humanitarianism in a world wracked by injustice. Described as "ideal instruments of mercy," the Binets are admirable aid workers but questionable parents (185). Sylvie's sense of inadequacy and shame are not justified; she has ordinary needs and desires, but these pale in comparison to her parents' larger mission. The elder Binets realize that Sylvie is not suited to their work, and they begin to prepare for Sylvie an alternative life in Seattle with her aunt while they continue their life-endangering work. The Binets' larger sense of moral duty overshadows their emotional responsibilities to their daughter.

The danger of their work comes to a head in 1934 after the Japanese invade Manchuria.[15] Sylvie's Latin tutor, Benjamin Li, with whom she has a quasi-sexual relationship,[16] is discovered to be secretly working with the Chinese resistance, a fact that Sylvie's father had known. In an echo of the Japanese occupation of Korea in *A Gesture Life,* Lee shows the brutality of the imperial Japanese army in Manchuria. The Japanese soldiers hold the Chinese and American missionaries and aid workers hostage as they try to exhort confessions from Li. After a Japanese officer murders the Chinese minister, Sylvie's father is given the choice to shoot Li himself and thereby save the rest of the mission. Even though Li's death is inevitable, he refuses, much like Hector refusing to kill the Chinese prisoner of war. The Japanese commander tries to force Li to confess by making him rape Sylvie's mother. When this fails to illicit a confession, the commander threatens to rape Sylvie himself. Sylvie's mother dies defending her, but Li caves after having his eyelids removed so that he would be forced to watch Sylvie's assault. Saved from rape, Sylvie escapes Manchuria with her life but not her family.

The impact of these events on Sylvie's psyche is absolute. Back in the United States, she begins a sexual relationship with a lonely older man, who, like Jake Barnes in Hemingway's *The Sun Also Rises,* has suffered a war injury that makes him unable to have intercourse. Together he and Sylvie drink opium and numb themselves to the world. Viewing her sexuality as an indication of "her ugly narcissism," Sylvie marries Ames Tanner, a deacon at her local church, who she thinks will "compel her into the wider world" much as her parents did (226). Their marriage is troubled, as Sylvie suffers multiple miscarriages and Ames blames her (and her sexuality) for this punishment. Sylvie is caught in a cycle of shame, and her needs are subsumed by Ames's work.

Despite his noble purpose, Ames Tanner's humanitarianism does not extend to his own wife. Like Orleanna Price in Barbara Kingsolver's *The Poisonwood Bible* (1998), Sylvie is married to a man whose missionary work supersedes the significance of a healthy marriage. *The Poisonwood Bible* is the inevitable comparison for this subplot of *The Surrendered.* Both novels focus on a missionary preacher and his troubled wife; unlike Nathan Price, however, Ames is not a zealot but simply a poor husband who is unable to meet his wife's emotional needs. For all their marital woes, Sylvie is drawn to Tanner for this hopefulness and chance at redemption, viewing him as "a beacon shining out from a dark shoreline" (127).

Lee draws further comparison to Kingsolver's novel not simply in the marriage of Ames and Sylvie Tanner but also through frequent allusions to missionary work in the Congo that connect Korean missionary work of the period to increasing imperial political interventions.[17] When Reverend Tanner arrives at New Hope, he gives a sermon to the orphans about his spiritual awakening after a nearly fatal illness: "I knew then that I had been living only a half life, and thus not a life at all, that all of my worldly knowledge and expertise and efforts were useful and valuable but only as a living devotion to the mercy of God and his Eternal Love. I had been delivered, as I hope you will be delivered, into a glorious new life" (127). Tanner's experience of Christian redemption is what Sylvie hopes for herself, even as she—like Hector and June—wrestles with the pain of living a "half life."

The damaged psyche of Sylvie Tanner is reflected in the orphans they encounter at New Hope. Reverend Tanner's job at New Hope is to facilitate American adoptions for the children, a mission that reflects American interest in atoning for the mistakes of the Korean War. The historian Arissa Oh noted in her study of the Korean origins of transnational adoptions in the United States that adoption became an extension of American humanitarianism after the end of the war: "If GI humanitarianism offered a way for Americans to salvage a moral victory out of the stalemate of the Korean War, then adopting a Korean orphan was a way for Americans to atone for abandoning—for orphaning—the land of her birth. Furthermore, the relationship between American parents and Korean children mirrored geopolitics by enacting the asymmetry that has characterized the neocolonial U.S.-Korea relationship since World War II."[18] While Tanner has been driven to Korean missionary work by his spiritual calling and his troubled marriage, his specific aims are to find the children "a glorious new life" in American Christian homes. Lee highlights the way the Tanners' missionary efforts reflect both the deep power imbalance between the countries and the moral guilt the Americans hold for the outcomes of this failed war. While preparing the children's adoption files, Sylvie begins to play the part of confessor, as the children come to her with their heart-wrenching personal war stories. Unable to sustain this role, Sylvie allows her husband to take it over, and she falls deeper into her morphine addiction.

Despite the children's fear of moving to a distant land with an unfamiliar culture, the stakes of not being adopted are realized by each child, for "nothing could be more terrifying than being passed over time and again and eventually being let back out into the ruined streets of Seoul, where there was little to earn in any legitimate trade" (163). June's difficult personality would seem to set her up for this abandoned fate, but the arrival of a middle-aged farm couple from Oregon, Mr. and Mrs. Stolz, looking to adopt six New Hope orphans briefly promises a new future for sullen June. Here, Lee is thinly veiling the allusion to the real Oregonian farm couple, Harry and Bertha Holt, who in 1955 adopted eight Korean orphans and brought four more to the United States for other families to adopt. This was the beginning of the Holts' mission of bringing Korean orphans to the United States and working to ease legislative barriers to international adoption. Their work was so successful, Oh wrote, that "in 1956, the Holts placed 191 orphans and established the Holt Adoption Program, which placed 2,587 Korean children with American families by 1961. Between 1955 and 1961, Holt placed the majority of Korean orphans in the United States."[19] Oh has argued further that the image of the Korean war orphan helped alter American attitudes toward Asian immigration. Orphans were not subject to the same immigration quotas that adult immigrants faced, which in turn allowed popular opinion toward Asian immigrants to shift. Lee, then, pinpoints the arrival of the Holts as a significant outcome of the aftermath of the Korean War.

Mrs. Stolz takes a liking to June, who is overwhelmed by a longing for her family. But when Mrs. Stolz touches the tortoiseshell hair clip given to June by Sylvie and calls June a "fluttering butterfly," June's passion breaks out, and she physically repulses both Stolzes and flees. Seeming to reject the role of delicate, fragile orphan, June lashes out to let her true self be revealed. Yet the "butterfly" also calls to mind Puccini's *Madame Butterfly.* While June seems as far removed from Cio-Cio San's character as possible, in some ways she, like Madame Butterfly, waits for her American love to return her affections and treat her as she deserves. Having rejected the Stolzes' offer, June indulges in a fantasy that she is adopted by Sylvie. Reflecting on her actions, June realizes that "she could not be a part of any other family again. In a different lifetime, she would have her parents back, her older brother and sister would be healthy, the twins happy and whole; but in this one she had been paired up, she and Sylvie aligned like twins themselves, if by one of them not quite acknowledged" (404–5). The relationship that June envisions with Sylvie is complex and in some ways contradictory. Wishing that Sylvie would adopt her, here June sees Sylvie not as a mother but as a twin or sister. Her desire for Sylvie extends far beyond a simple need for a parent.

Having made this life-altering decision, June, despite having not eaten, feels her hunger as "more like purity than privation" (405). Lee is a novelist preoccupied with the symbolic value of food, and in *The Surrendered,* it is June's hunger that most poetically illustrates this common motif in Lee's work. The novel opens with the near starvation of the refugees during the war. June catches a woman hiding food, and her reaction is first shame and then anger; hunger drives people to blind hatred. June contemplates killing herself and her siblings to prevent slow death from starvation. At New Hope the orphans still struggle with their experience of hunger. Hector observes one boy trying to break his habit of eating bugs he has found (117); another child fills her emotional emptiness by drinking too much water, a trick she learned while starving during the war. Although June feels a sense of constant hunger, she intentionally denies herself food as a demonstration of control over her life: "The hunger. It had come for June again. . . . But this time, she wasn't hiding or running from it; she was inviting it along in a kind of dance, as a partner, a companion that would mark her every move. She knew that hunger would clarify her mind, strip away all extraneous thought, and leave her with the focus of pure, unswerving will" (432). June's anorexia is about self-control and expression of her force of will. Given how little power over her life she has had to this point, denying herself food gives June a feeling of triumph over her bodily needs, triumph over that past horror that tormented her during the war.

Whereas June's addiction is meant to sharpen her senses, Sylvie's addiction to morphine is meant to dull hers. Having first administered morphine in Manchuria to an injured missionary, Sylvie is an addict when she arrives at New Hope. Hector recognizes the needle marks on her ankle, and as with her lover Jim, Sylvie's sexual relationship with Hector includes drug use. An alcoholic himself, Hector has a desire for Sylvie that is also a sort of addiction: "He didn't understand then how deeply he needed her, that he loved not just her sharp wants and carnality but how tightly bound up those were with her decency and beauty and goodness; she was exalted and flawed, someone who required as much grace and succor as she herself readily offered, someone both he and June desperately needed, a mother and a lover and a kind of child, too. That first time they made love, when she opened the back door of the cottage for him, she had fallen upon him as if she'd thrown herself from a parapet, with the grave force of both will and surrender" (323). Hector's description of the mixed roles Sylvie plays in the fantasy lives of both Hector and June demonstrates the ambiguous nature of their relationships with Sylvie, who, for all of this description, remains ephemeral. Whereas June is marked by sheer force of will, Lee lets Sylvie embody this paradox of strength and vulnerability. Her suicidal behavior is cast as driven by her force of will—but unlike June, her will is to surrender to the horrors of life.

June's desire for Sylvie is as strong as Hector's, and like Hector, one night she loses control:

> Here was the only beauty in the world. And then one night June could not help herself; she pulled back the blanket as if it were the frail lead of an antique book. Her hands crept to Sylvie's throat, where her nightgown opened, and undid the mother-of-pearl buttons that ran down to the hem; she took them one by one, the near half of the nightgown falling away,

> exposing the whole length of Sylvie now to the cold night air. June touched the belly, grazed the lowest rib, the small, flattish breast no fuller than her own. The nipple pushed up between her fingers, as dense as clay, and without knowing what she was doing she put her mouth over it, closing her eyes. She couldn't breathe again, her heart as if collapsed in her chest, this tiny leaden node, poised for Sylvie to protest, to stir. But she did not. Nor did she when June's hand slid down and nestled in the burning cup of her long legs, not moving, nor stirring, neither wanting the other to wake. (346)

As in Hector's first sexual encounter with Sylvie, here the line between lover and mother is blurred. Lee's specific use of "mother-of-pearl" foregrounds June's suckling of Sylvie's breast, an act that can be maternal or sexual but that is blurred here. If Sylvie is viewed as an older mother figure, her sexual relationship with the teenage June in this scene is perverse and taboo. Stephanie Hsu noted that their relationship "both queers and crips the power relationship between the humanitarian worker and the recipient of aid."[20] In turn, June initiates this encounter while Sylvie is heavily sedated by morphine and in a deep sleep. Although Lee concludes with "neither wanting the other to wake," Sylvie's debilitated state makes consent ambiguous at best.

June is confused by their encounter and is afraid that giving in to her desire ruined her future with Sylvie. She is determined to "only be a good daughter" (388) by demonstrating to Reverend Tanner that she is "a worthy girl at core" (391). June's performance is successful, but she has misread the situation. After breaking her fast too rapidly with Sylvie's dinner one night, June vomits, and Sylvie takes on a maternal role, praising her for being "the girl I always believed you were" and saying that she foresees a life "full of love's riches" in June's future because of her capacity for love (449). Inspired by June's performance as an innocent child, Sylvie clearly does not want to acknowledge June's true complexity; instead she assumes the role of a benevolent teacher. Sylvie then bequeaths to June her beloved and battered copy of *A Memory of Solferino* as a parting gift. Shocked by the conclusive end of her fantasy of adoption, June turns to "right hard stone" in Sylvie's embrace, and Sylvie is dumbfounded.

Failing to find a mother or lover in Sylvie, June finds another person to act as substitute family. June and another outcast orphan named Min had taken to sleeping together in the chapel that Hector built as a way to avoid bullies. United to June in his desire to leave with the Tanners, Min reminds June of her younger brother. Once she realizes that their fantasies are mere delusions, she and Min begin to burn their few possessions as a sign of their independence. After she allows Min to throw Sylvie's book into the fire, June snatches it out again, burning her hands. Full of despair, together June and Min try to commit suicide by setting the small chapel on fire. The love triangle between Hector, Sylvie, and Tanner is exposed, and Tanner confronts Sylvie and Hector about their affair moments before the chapel explodes. They all rush to save the children, and Hector sees flames envelop Sylvie, Tanner, and Min. Desiring his own death, Hector is saved by June, who pulls his body out of the chapel to safety. They both survive because of June's will to live, much to Hector's regret.

June immigrates to the United States not as an adopted war orphan but as a (post)war bride, with Hector marrying her in name only. These dual identities, Oh argued, helped redefine the cultural stereotype of the Asian immigrant: "Together, the war orphan, war bride, and model minority offered a new image of Asians in the United States: anti-Communist, assimilable, conforming to American values, and therefore contributing to a stronger nation. Of these, the Korean orphan was the best kind of immigrant. Free of the potentially subversive adult refugee or the sexual threat of the war bride, and full of the promise of childhood, she was the worthiest of immigrants, deserving of entering the 'circle of care' provided by both the nuclear and the national American family. She was the ideal future citizen, at once a model minority and a model immigrant."[21] June, war orphan, appears to fulfill the "model minority" expectation, as at the end of her life she is a successful antiques dealer in New York City. Yet the novel also confirms her status of war bride, with its potential subversive "sexual threat." Despite a marriage of convenience, June conceives a child with Hector in an episode that echoes her encounter with Sylvie; June mounts a drunken Hector while he sleeps, "leaving him with the feeling that he'd been not so much used as robbed" (316). June's cold personal manner, her dysfunctional nonnuclear family, and her bisexuality all work to undermine her "model minority" appearance; her multiple acts of rape are antithetical to it. In this opposition to one stereotype, however, Lee risks casting June as a dragon lady, a dangerous sexual predator.

However, June's complicated psychology keeps this potential interpretation from taking hold. Although June manipulates Hector into following her to Europe to search for Nicholas by playing upon his need to torture himself with Sylvie's memory, she is also hopeful that she can trigger a real relationship between her son and his father. In traveling to Italy with June to see the church at Solferino, Hector shows great mercy toward June in her last days. It is Hector who discovers that "Nicholas" is an imposter and then actively conceals the bitter truth from June. When Hector tracks down the man who has been extorting money from June via postcards, he is struck by his beauty:

> Nick was very handsome, but in a perfectly original way. At the orphanage there had been a number of mixed-blood kids, a natural consequence of

> war. They were sometimes teased or shunned by the others, but to Hector they looked like no one in creation with their wide, petaling eyes and buttery, earthen coloring. Yet despite their beauty and hybrid vigor he couldn't help but see them as somehow vulnerable, too, doomed to their singularity, their species of one, which mirrored, strangely, how he had always felt inside. They could also appear so different from moment to moment, shape-shift when not even meaning to, as Nick was now, the mixing inside him veiling and unveiling this feature and that, depending on the angle, or the light. (359)

This passage is perhaps Lee's most explicit fetishization of the mixed-race child. From Mitt in *Native Speaker,* to Theresa and Jack Battle in *Aloft,* to Reg in *On Such a Full Sea,* Lee's work presents the figure of the multiracial child as uniquely beautiful with subversive potential but also racially confused—and frequently doomed like the "tragic mulatto" trope of nineteenth-century literature. Of these characters, however, June's Nicholas—and the man pretending to be Nicholas—is the most bereft of clear identity. This Nicholas is also vaguely dangerous in his ability to pick up and cast off identities. Hector finds this appealing but also unsettling, as he sees his own ill-fitting identity reflected in what he projects upon these children.

Hector, sensing a moral lack in Nicholas, considers not telling June that he located him, but Nicholas goes to June himself, and she does not indicate that she realizes this man is not her son. When "Nick" confesses the truth to Hector, that June's premonition of Nicholas's death after that midnight phone call from the hospital was correct and that he had assumed June's son's identity, Hector forces "Nick" to continue the masquerade to set June's mind at ease as she seeks absolution from her rejection of his hospital-bed plea. The force of June's will is so strong that she manages to reunite and reconcile with her already dead son.

The imposter does, however, return to June the copy of *A Memory of Solferino* that her son took from her when he left home. A gift from the Binets to Sylvie and then given by Sylvie to June, this book travels alongside most of the active plots in the novel. Written by J. Henry Dunant, founder of the Red Cross and winner of the first Nobel Peace Prize, in 1862, the book details the brutality of the Austro-Sardinian War of 1859. Hsu noted how *The Surrendered* uses Dunant's text to investigate the role of the reader in understanding humanitarian crisis:

> Accordingly, Sylvie's copy of Dunant's text engenders multiple and overlapping modes of readerly interpellation among Lee's characters that further

> destabilize their social roles: Hector experiences a moment of "pure self-erasure" when he inserts himself into the role of a dying soldier (141); June, who uses the book as an English primer, imagines Sylvie to be the eyewitness author (249); and the last time Hector and Sylvie make love, on the night of the orphanage fire, *Memory*'s rhetorical structure seems finally to have replicated itself in the narrative—"It was as if an entire army of him had fallen on her, overrunning her in waves" (458). In fact, the novel frequently invokes this intertext in a manner that resembles Sylvie's meditative reading practice, as if aiming for the humanitarian indifference to suffering, for the sublimation of specific injury and personal identity that even Sylvie finds impossible to achieve.[22]

All of the central characters of the novel work to find ways to access or deny the extreme traumas they have experienced, and by reading this novel, the reader is likewise forced to associate or disassociate with the horrors represented within. The specificity of individual human suffering stands in the context of collective horror, but only in individual experience can it be perceived. Novels operate on the necessity of the specific as a means to understanding the larger scale of human suffering.

In the midst of an argument, Hector tells Sylvie that her book—and her philosophy of philanthropy—is a lie: "I thought it was about showing mercy to the helpless, to the innocent. But I think that book of yours is worthless. In fact, it's worse than that. It's a lie. It's changed nothing and never will" (430). He is angered by her willingness to comfort others but her refusal to accept true connection, for providing hope through her person without ever truly committing herself to anyone. Hector and Sylvie argue once more before the fire in the chapel takes her life. Again berating her for not matching his dependency, Hector tells her that "hope is your drug," to which Sylvie replies with a memory of her mother telling her that nothing was worse than when "loving mercy" was "misspent" (472).

Mercy and human compassion are dominant themes of the novel. Near the beginning these themes are laid out in the story that a man tells on the road full of fleeing refugees. In this tale no one stops to give water to a dying old woman. Berating the refugees for their lack of compassion, the man gives a speech: "I am talking about decency. About something as basic as that. We could offer her only the smallest comfort. She died shortly thereafter but, my God, she was alone and afraid and in misery. Who in this room would ever wish anyone an end like that?" (7). At the conclusion of the novel, Hector is more than decent and merciful to June, a woman he has many reasons to despise. In addition to the large acts of kindness he performs in taking her to Italy and tracking down her "son," Hector takes on the responsibilities of little intimacies, such as administering the morphine that lessens June's pain from her cancer. As merciful as he is to June, he, like Sylvie in Korea, cannot be merciful to himself. Blaming himself for Sylvie's death by the curse of his existence, he imagines a preposterous alternative life for Sylvie and June in which Sylvie is a happy grandmother to June's happy children (380). So caught up in his own self-torture, Hector cannot realize the absurdity of such a fantasy for women like Sylvie and June. Blinded by his own lack of self-worth, he is unable to assess fairly the reality of their characters. In penance, he takes June to Solferino.

The church at Solferino is an ossuary, with the bones of the dead from the Battle of Solferino decorating the church. When Sylvie first visits the church with her parents, she only gradually sees the skeletal remains: "And then she heard them, as if she were on the stage peering out at the audience of a macabre opera house, the coaly voids of countless eyes speaking to her all at once. . . . *Look at us,* they said to her, in a single voice. *We were never divine*" (194–95). Sylvie, haunted by the spectacle of so many unknown dead, hears their ghostly voices. When Hector finally sees the chapel, he recognizes that the cross above the altar resembles the one he had built for Sylvie when she first arrived at New Hope. Hector is surprised that the bones are out in the open, "touched only by time" (483). His voice is transformed as he whispers to June, "*It is beautiful. . . . This is our place*" (483). Hector is speaking to Sylvie as much as to June, and his astonishment harkens back to his feelings when he completed the chapel at the orphanage. Having feared that his dark, concrete chapel looked like a "tomb for the living," he had added windows, asymmetrical and irregular. Sylvie's joy at the church had made him almost ready to reengage with the world. With June's death undeniable, Hector's fate remains ambiguous. Whether he views the church at Solferino as another living tomb or whether he is able to reimagine his life as ordinary and driven by choice rather than fate remains unclear.

June too hears a voice in Solferino: a "phantom took its form in a woman's voice: *I'm here, I'm here, I'm here*" (369).[23] She interprets it first as the voice of Sylvie, then that of an embodied form of her cancer, and ultimately as her own voice. The voice torments her, but June is pure will through the pain: "One need not surrender. It wasn't always the case. She wasn't crazy. Although she could hardly distinguish anymore between waking and sleep, . . . she felt sure she was right about this. She was almost certain that she could hold on for a long time, maybe indefinitely, croon along with the voice ringing in her head and thus stay hinged to the present. Never let herself go" (370). Whereas Hector views his fated immortality as a curse, June thinks her will could grant her longer life, that she can overpower death by sheer determination. But her stomach cancer is consuming her; her organ of hunger will cause her death. June realizes that she will die and contemplates the existence of an afterlife where she might be reunited with her family and the Tanners: "Her parents had not practiced any faith, nor had she, but it seemed reasonable that there should be simple questions now about all that one did in one's life, and whether those commissions were on balance decent, humane" (379). This implicit question, like that of Hector's fate, remains unanswered: How does one know if the balance of one's decency or humanity outweighs the worst of human nature?

Just as the novel opens with the promise of closure, *The Surrendered* ends with the promise of a beginning. Despite June's impending death, the novel concludes with the teenage June running for the last car of the train that saves her during the war: "She could not look back. She loved them all but she knew if she looked back she was done. She would come to a stop. And she did not want to stop, not just yet. Not now. To crave anything, alas, is to crave time. She was simply hungry for more. The wheels of the last car squealed and flashed; it was accelerating, about to pull away. In defiance she leaned forward and cried out, suspending her breath, and reached for the dark edge of the door. The world fell away. Someone had pulled her up. Borne her in. She was off her feet, alive" (484). Here, in the final words of the novel, is the key to June's steely, determined character. Hungry for more life, she uses her will power to cut the emotional and physical barriers to her chance at life, finally explaining her "effortlessly monstrous ability, as if she could simply pluck from her heel a spur called love, her own cool blood the quickest antidote" (335). Far from unable to love, June's "monstrous ability" comes from her desire to survive. To the end, June is tenacious of life.

CHAPTER 6

"A special conviction of imagination"

On Such a Full Sea (2014)

Chang-rae Lee's latest novel, *On Such a Full Sea,* was published in January 2014 and signaled the most radical change in Lee's quest to "widen the stage" of his art.[1] His move into dystopian fantasy in the novel at first seems unexpected given the intimate and carefully wrought literary realism of his early work. Yet Lee's move toward a form that is often dismissed as "genre fiction" has recent precedents from critically established writers such as Kazuo Ishiguro, Colson Whitehead, and many others. As was the case with these authors, Lee's critical success afforded him, at this stage in his career, an opportunity to take greater creative risks while continuing his interrogation of identity and subjectivity. The critical response to Lee's latest novel has been mixed. While many critics have exuberantly praised it for pushing the formal boundaries of his earlier work, several have been more harshly critical—for example, Michiko Kakutani, who despite championing Lee's earlier work, wrote that *On Such a Full Sea* "often reads like a ham-handed mash-up of Aldous Huxley's *Brave New World* and Suzanne Collins's *The Hunger Games*"[2] While other critics have drawn similar comparisons, albeit in more complimentary tones, what Kakutani alluded to here is the way Lee merges a premise and plot belonging to young adult "genre fiction" with experimental narration more characteristic of "literary fiction."

Yet Lee embraces this sort of so-called high- and lowbrow mixing from the very start of the novel; the epigraphs are from William Shakespeare's *Julius Caesar* (from which Lee took his title) and the rock band Journey's "Only the Young." *On Such a Full Sea* takes place in a near future in which the world order has been reorganized following what appears to be gradual environmental collapse.[3] The novel begins in the suggestively named city of B-Mor, a Chinese labor colony that was imported wholesale to live in the remains of the abandoned city of Baltimore and raise fish for the affluent Charter cities. The irony of the city's name is that the citizens of B-Mor have no desire to be anything more than passive laborers and consumers; they are grateful not to be in the open country without the security of their limited but protected space. Christopher T. Fan noted that Lee's fictional world is the result of "a process that can only be described as neoliberalization: either an unlivable cult of individualism, or an existential resignation and total dependency."[4] Lee commented that "the scariest dystopias are those of the soul."[5] The collective consciousness of the community of B-Mor narrates the story of the teen heroine, Fan. Living isolated in stratified communities with limited educational opportunity and social mobility, the pregnant Fan, a talented fish tank diver, leaves the safety of her family and community to search for her missing boyfriend Reg, who has been taken by the authorities because he, unlike the rest of the human population, tests negative for the cancerlike diseases called only "Cs." Fan becomes a legend to the community for her confounding act of leaving the safety of home and inspires a short-lived resistance movement in B-Mor.

Originally intending to write a "big, sprawling book about China,"[6] Lee visited a factory near Shenzhen to conduct research about the women who live and work there. Although he soon abandoned the project, Lee reported that "something about that factory and its community kept gnawing at me, not just notions about the individuals and their labors and how they thought of themselves but what their communal sensibility might be, a certain ethos that might develop with enclosure."[7] In a brief essay appearing on his publisher's Web site, Lee explained that the novel evolved organically rather than from a self-conscious desire to write dystopian fiction:

> Certainly when I was young I was an admirer of such classic novels of dystopia as *1984* and *Fahrenheit 451*, but, in fact, in writing this book I didn't want any models of the genre to guide me. I was simply working the way I have always worked, which is to imagine characters who find themselves at a pivotal moment in their lives, characters who are questioning their place in their families and communities and, in turn, those communities' place in the wider world. In this regard, I consider *On Such a Full Sea* to be more of an extension of my previous novels than any radical departure. This is particularly true if one considers the so-called immigrant narratives of my earlier novels, which I've always felt were essentially dystopian in nature; for what does such a fiction describe if not a world in which the beliefs and practices are unfamiliar and sometimes backward, in which the morality

> is skewed, and whose every civil contour feels wrong, if only to its newly arrived hero, who must venture into and negotiate his way through a brave new world. In a dystopian fiction, we, the readers, are enlisted to experience this "adventure"; we are the new arrivals on the scene of a seemingly bizarre civilization, which of course has closer—and thus more unsettling—correspondences to our own than we ever anticipated. This is how I conceived of *On Such a Full Sea*.[8]

In an interview in *Vulture,* Lee put it more pithily: "All immigrant novels are dystopian novels. They're just not dystopias for most of the readers."[9]

In interviews Lee has shown signs of anxiety about *On Such a Full Sea* being dismissed as dystopian genre fiction. In an interview with the online literary magazine *Rumpus,* he noted being especially pleased that the writers and critics focused on the first-person-plural narration rather than the switch to "dystopian stuff."[10] In another interview, Lee was asked if he is a fan of dystopian lit. He replied, "I'm not automatically drawn to tales because they're dystopian. The classics from Orwell and Huxley, and contemporary works by McCarthy, Atwood, and Ishiguro are excellent because they expose our condition, certain possibilities of human expression and conduct, and not just because they're set in some imagined or futuristic realm. The altered context of these realms should surely be diverting, but it's how the context forms and deforms the characters that compels me as a reader. Otherwise it's just fancy scenery and essentially repetitive episodes."[11] Lee has subtly but consistently distanced himself from the ways he is being categorized and chafed at the novel's being reduced to genre alone.[12] Although the dystopian label is determined largely on the futuristic setting of the novel, the book reads more like a surreal twist on the present than a truly divergent future. The narrators reflect on the limitations of their story in a way that is useful for the readers of this novel: "Imagination might not be limitless. It's still tethered to the universe of what we know, and as wild as our dreams might be, we can't help but read them with the same grounded circumspection that guided our forebears when they mapped out our walls" (109). Wild and inventive, the reality of the novel is only quasi-futuristic, revealing the follies of contemporary American life.

Another reason for distancing *On Such a Full Sea* from genre literature may be the critical backlash Lee encountered when breaking out of expectations for "ethnic fiction" with his third novel, *Aloft*. So what can be viewed as the author distancing himself from "genre" labels in interviews is less about the actual formal shift and more about the constant need to resist the presumptive categorization of his work. This seems especially legitimate given the way his novels have been regularly—in the popular and academic criticism—held to the confines of being by an ethnic American writer, the representative Korean American novelist. Lee instead has emphasized the progressive broadening of his point of view in each subsequent novel: "I've been widening my perspective with each book, although I didn't have any conscious intention of doing so. Perhaps this comes simply from aging and maturing, the natural shift of focus from private selves to seeing those figures and consciousnesses in a broader context. Perhaps I am more interested in context and circumstance as I go along: how the larger forces and influences shape one's being."[13]

On Such a Full Sea is presented as a work of folklore, albeit one from a fictional culture. Reflecting on the unusual perspective of the novel, Lee noted, "'We' can be anything from a sort of chorus, omniscient and perhaps moralizing, to something more particular, even 'individual' in sensibility, with biases and desires, or can at times seem confused and unreliable, or else sustained by pure hope and conjecture. I enjoyed exploring these fluctuations and decided not to disqualify any. And I found they made Fan's adventures more interesting to me, because, after all, it's as much about the telling as it is the tale."[14] Although the perspective of the novel often seems like one narrator using "we" to mean like-minded people, at others times it seems like a genuine "we"—the collective narration group of scholars of Fan, the legend and mystery. While an unusual formal choice, it does underscore the communal dynamic of B-Mor, a place where individuality does not matter and only the success and stability of the group are important. B-Mor is represented in terms of kinship with the entire community operating like a family. When Fan breaks with this way of life, she inspires confusion and longing in those she has left behind.

This is a novel about storytelling. Lee creates a world where the act of reconstructing the myth of Fan is a common cultural act and one loaded with rebellious potential. Jiayang Fan wrote, "Because silent submission to the directorate is implicit, and most of oral history serves as a propagandistic form of self-pacification, Fan's disappearance is peculiar."[15] Early in the novel, the narrators describe Uncle Kellen, a truck driver who would "talk story" about the history of B-Mor (68). As in Maxine Hong Kingston's 1976 novel *Woman Warrior,* "talking story" allows for the subversive tales of the past to survive through the sanitation of official histories. Lee writes, "His [Uncle Kellen's] stories weren't exactly the ones you studied in school or watched vids of at the historical museum, the oft-documented stuff about how by dint of their collective will and the discipline of their leaders in keeping everyone focused on the job the originals transformed the desperate nothingness about them" (68–69). Instead, Uncle Kellen's stories reveal the true history of colonization in B-Mor. Like this early storyteller, the narrators of Fan's tale are really providing a transgressive counterstory to the seeming cultural uniformity of B-Mor by presenting Fan as a mythic trigger for the eventual uprising of the resistance.

In reviewing the book for the *New York Times,* Andrew Sean Greer found Lee's combination of "genre pleasures" with the creepy "communal voice" of the narration successful.[16] Maureen Corrigan, writing for National Public Radio, found it "off-putting."[17] Yet both critics, in antithetical reviews of the novel, noted that the heroine Fan "remains a cipher" to the reader because of the nature of the narration. There is undeniably an emotional distance from this heroine, and while the popular critical preoccupation has (so far) focused on this as a failing or misfire in the novel, what is most interesting is the way Lee's amorphous heroine is reminiscent of earlier female figures in his works. From the mystery that is Ahjuma in Lee's debut *Native Speaker,* to the enigma of the comfort woman K in *A Gesture Life,* to the absent presence of Daisy Battle in *Aloft,* Lee's work is filled with mysterious, unknowable women—all of them Asian or Asian American. For this reason Fan is an unlikely heroine. Lee sets the reader up for a form that demands a powerful dystopian teen heroine and yet refuses to follow through with expectations. Fan's quiet moral strength—one that does not rely on violence, physical strength, or even charisma—Lee seems to counter, demands respect. Yet even as Lee resists fulfilling genre conventions in his heroine, Fan continues to serve as a totem for her community.

Lee has discussed the symbolic weight of Fan's character in interviews. When asked if he drew inspiration from Herman Melville's *Moby-Dick,* Lee related Fan to perhaps that most famous symbol of American literature, the great white whale: "The whale itself has no consciousness. The consciousness and presence that it is given come from those around it. I don't want to try to elevate or make anything grandiose, but Fan has the same sort of role. She's elemental. There's something about her that is absent of human consciousness in the ways we normally get human consciousness in a maximal way in fiction. She is also a kind of canvas that we all want to write on; at least, the people of B-Mor do. There is something about her elemental quality that is probably a little Melvillian."[18] Fan's consciousness, so integral to most fictional works and particularly important to an author who, like Lee, specializes in detailed portraits of individual human psychology, is intentionally left blank so that Lee can focus instead on the collective consciousness of a society.

For all the novelty of first-person-plural narration (and it is unusual and often compelling to read), the end result is that the characterization of Fan is very much like those of enigmatic women of the limited and unreliable first-person narrations of Lee's earliest works. One of the most disturbing characters in Lee's canon is K, the comfort woman upon whom the narrator of *A Gesture*

Life, Doc Hata, projects his desires. In her critique of *A Gesture Life,* Kandice Chuh argued that in Lee's emphasis on Korea as a postcolonial nation (as embodied through the relationship of K and the Japanese-raised Hata), the novel fails to represent or acknowledge American neocolonization.[19] *On Such a Full Sea,* however, engages directly with U.S. neocolonial projects. In fact, Lee breaks down geographical barriers as Fan is descended from environmental refugees from China brought to the United States to work in isolated labor camps. Globalized labor is brought home; Lee transposes contemporary exploitation of Chinese labor onto U.S. soil in a literal labor colony. In this way Lee simultaneously critiques contemporary American neocolonization (through neoliberal economic policy run to extreme conclusions) while riffing on the history of Chinese labor in building U.S. wealth. The creation of a future world of extreme racialized class stratification suggests that Lee, through this dystopian form, wants to expose the economic injustice that provides for the American present.

Through Fan's episodic adventures, Lee presents three different societies existing within the territory of the former United States: the Charter elite; the laboring B-Mor middle class; and the abandoned people of the lawless "open counties." The novel begins a hundred years after the emigration of a whole city from "New China," which faced environmental collapse. Settling into what was once Baltimore, the citizens of the new B-Mor community labor to provide "clean" food by farming pristine fish and produce for the wealthy Charter cities. B-Mor was created as a solution to Charter fears of environmental contamination and C-disease, which makes B-Mor's economy entirely powered by the fickle demand for these luxury goods by the Charter cities.[20] When rumor spreads that fish may be related to the near-universal C-disease, the demand for B-Mor produce breaks down, and the precarious social fabric of B-Mor erodes in tandem.

The city of Baltimore, along with Lee's interest in writing a book about Chinese factory towns, spurred the creation of *On Such a Full Sea:*

> Around the time I was backing away from the China novel, I was travelling between New York and Washington on the train, which goes through a derelict section of Baltimore. On the return trip, we passed by again, and again I saw that sad neighborhood, which I realized I'd been seeing throughout my adult life. Decades, and really nothing had changed. Maybe it was my frustration, my feeling of powerlessness, but I was suddenly struck by a very strange idea about re-populating this and other abandoned urban areas like it all in one stroke, boom, say with a homogenous colony of foreigners. The idea was unlikely but conceptually exciting, and the more I thought about it, the more I realized that a component of my interest in China was an

> anxiety about the decline of American power and status. So I fiddled with various basic scenarios, testing them to see which provoked the most compelling questions, and a picture of a kind of labor colony began to emerge. But to make the scenario plausible—there was no way re-populating could happen anytime soon—I realized I had to set this colony within a very different future and a very different America, one that might tolerate and even need such settlers.[21]

That Lee must stretch to imagine a future time when such immigrants would be welcomed as a boon to the American economy is disheartening, but not more so than the imagined place that would accommodate colonization. Lee's interest in and anxiety about the rise of China and the decline of America, then, becomes mapped on the very real decline and stagnation of neighborhoods in Baltimore, a predominately black city.

As in most American stories of immigrants conquering new land, the narrators downplay the existence of people already living in the remains of Baltimore, but the novel's treatment of this history reveals the racial coding within B-Mor. While the "originals" from New China thrived in B-Mor, the "descendants of nineteenth-century African slaves and twentieth-century laborers from Central America and even bands of twenty-first century urban-nostalgics . . . inexorably declined and finally disappeared" (19). With this assurance of "inexorable" disappearance comes later information about the seizing of "native"-owned businesses and property by the early governing body of B-Mor (69). Those "natives" not driven out of B-Mor appear to have been assimilated into the stock of the "originals," as the systematic tracking of "mixed" peoples for special medical monitoring is instituted. Fan's boyfriend, Reg, is one of these "mixed" people, and his "amazing head of Afro-type hair" becomes the model for popular hairstyles among the youth of B-Mor during the resistance movement despite the racism that pervades the culture (66).

It is suggested that Reg's "mixed" genes are the cause of his rumored exceptional status as the only person in B-Mor who is "C-free" (64). While no one is certain why Reg has been taken from the community, those in B-Mor believe that he has been taken for medical research. The discussion of C-disease is perhaps the best indicator of the class stratification in the novel. Death from C is inevitable for most, but rather than operate as the great equalizer, healthcare treatment varies by economic status. While people in the Charters use their financial resources to delay the inevitable, the options for those in B-Mor are limited. As the narrators say, "There is no leaping of worlds in this world" (51). The superiority and confidence the narrators evince when speaking of

B-Mor give way to stark inequity and reveal the extent to which this society is constructed as fully in service to upholding the elite class.

B-Mor is defined by its stagnation and inertia, a commentary on the deadening of the American middle class. Lee noted, "The B-Mor people have the middle-class trappings—decent enough food, some health care even if it is second-rate, but what they don't have is a certain kind of freedom. And I don't just mean political freedom. They've accepted and made a bargain in trading a life of safety for a suppression of their destiny. . . . there is something soulful that dies in that, I think. And also something about imagination that gets diminished."[22] B-Mor, the narrators admit, was "of a design unsustainable," and it is this knowledge, they suggest, that leads to the interest in Fan: "Which is why we needed Fan, in both idea and person. For within her was the one promise that could deliver us, the seed of all our futures, Charters' and B-Mors' and even the shunned souls out in the counties" (104). Fan, the idea, provides B-Mor with an imaginative alternative to the reality of the structures of their lives.

Her act of leaving their safe community confuses and fascinates them. That she first poisoned the fish she so loved before leaving causes grief, but also the interpretation that she did so "to save us and B-Mor" (98). While this conclusion seems convoluted, it suggests the narrators' desire to cast Fan in the role of prophet and even savior despite the community's lack of religious belief: "Fan . . . would have no real idea what the cost of transgressing any specific doctrine would be, religious or philosophical, as we in B-Mor pretty much practice none; other than an undying habit of pragmatic attention and action, there is no overarching system we subscribe to anymore, no devotion to a deity or origin story, no antique Eastern or Western assertions of goodness and badness to guide us" (147). Having replaced religion, philosophy, and moral law with the law of collective stability, the narrators' assertion of Fan's promise of deliverance reinforces the mystical, almost religious role Fan is meant to play. In addition to an imaginative break from the collective to follow her individual destiny, she carries another promise of salvation, for literally "within her" is Reg's baby, a baby that may also hold the genetic key to life without C-disease. Fan's baby may be the "seed of all our futures." Like a futuristic Virgin Mary, a young and pregnant Fan embarks on a journey that may lead to literal human salvation.

Fan's journey is filled with perils. She is hit by a car on her trip through the open counties, taken in by a clan of murderous circus performers, and brought to a settlement called the Smokes located somewhere in Appalachia. Each new episode provides opportunities for Fan to make moral choices, and she consistently chooses to do good in bad circumstances while continuing on with her mission. Life in the Smokes is filled with the expected Appalachian details: the people are dirty and have bad teeth; they live in the equivalent of shanties; there are many fatherless children; and they listen to "old-time fiddle music" (106). The narrators dwell on the aggression and desperation of the Smokes but also note the easy laughter among the people that is not the case in B-Mor. As in Lee's earlier novels, there is sentimental emphasis on the authenticity of human companionship in the midst of poverty and nostalgia for the simplicity of having nothing to fear losing. In spite of the fact that life is cruel and difficult among this desperate class of people, they share a human connection that is in sharp contrast to life in the Charters and in B-Mor.

The leader of the settlement is a man named Quig, whose former life as a veterinarian in the Charters now qualifies him as a doctor in the wasteland of the Smokes. Once a comfortable Charter family man, Quig loses his business since pets (like the fish of B-Mor) are considered dangerous to human health. Quig's family turns to drug dealing as a way to maintain their lifestyle. Eventually his wife and daughter are murdered by thieves on drugs after the family leaves the safety of the Charter community. Quig's fall from grace shows that the economic security of even the Charters could be as easily destroyed as that of B-Mor.

Quig is the center of the economy in the Smokes, where his clinic is run on bartering with any available resources, including sex and, as in the case of Fan, child slavery. Quig is, at best, a morally suspect individual, and the tension grows as the narrators present Fan as at the mercy of this unknown man. Because Quig determines his medical care based not on need but on ability to pay with goods, Fan seems particularly vulnerable to abuse and exploitation. But she makes herself valuable by improving the ticketing of Quig's clinic and helping to alleviate some of the suffering that surrounds her. In addition Quig frequently intervenes on Fan's behalf with less charitable people in the settlement who resent her race and middle-class status: "The Charters were much more exalted settlements but they might as well be constructed up in the clouds; there was no way a counties person could even dream of residing there. But a place like B-Mor, with its safe, clean streets and full employment and the promise of a gentle end, was a theoretically attainable and thus resented possibility to them. One need not even mention its legacy of foreign settlers, which, of course, was expressed in Fan's face and name, and could only catalyze certain feelings of unfairness and displacement, whether they were justified or not" (82). The seeming attainability of a middle-class life, Lee suggests, causes greater resentment among the impoverished than does the blatant inequity of how much the wealthy elite have for themselves. Lee generously delineates the intersection of class and racism within this group. Though unjustified, racism and nativism are the results of a sense of class "displacement" among those on the lowest rungs of the economic ladder, which rightly places the blame on those at the top who sustain this system of disparity to begin with—and benefit from the displaced resentment that Fan must face.

Quig, originating from the most elite class, shows no such prejudice, and yet he ultimately betrays and exploits Fan more than the racist, but powerless, masses at the settlement do. After Fan saves him from a murderous family of acrobats intent on serving him up as dog food, Quig gives Fan to a Charter couple in return for well-water drilling equipment and medicine that would prolong the life of a settlement child. Quig is a pragmatist, and there is no room for sentimentality where Fan is concerned, so she is left behind on the Charter estate in payment for the goods Quig needs. The dynamics of the Charter estate are echoes of those of plantation life where the wealthy whites are served by domestics of color. Fan is in fact a slave, having been paid for by "Mister Leo" and "Miss Cathy." Reassured that she is to be trained as a housekeeper, Fan meets Mala, who, like Ahjuma in *Native Speaker* and Rosario in *Aloft,* is a live-in servant to a wealthy family. Mala has a family living in the counties whom she sees every twenty days for a one-day visit. Like many immigrant workers, Mala sends her earnings home to support her family. Like Fan, Mala is of Asian descent but not New Chinese, as other Asian groups had emigrated to form labor colonies like B-Mor. But these other Asian immigrant groups, the narrators note, did not last "because there was trouble integrating them with our clans" (172). In fact, the narrators indicate that the conflict was more violent than the first encounter with "natives" upon arrival. For all this acknowledgment of interethnic conflict, Fan, however, "couldn't help but feel an affinity for this woman" who labors like her friends and family. Throughout the novel Fan is able to transcend ethnic and cultural difference to see the common humanity of those she meets.

Fan's peace with Mala is short-lived, as the full horrors of the Charter mansion come to the forefront. Fan discovers that she is one in a long line of teenaged Asian girls to be brought to live there, and Mala's role in grooming these girls is questioned. As with Quig before her, Mala's kindness to Fan does not mean that she will not ultimately do what is in her own best interest. Before long, Mister Leo's predatory interest in Fan leads to his attempted rape of the girl. Only the intervention of his wife, Miss Cathy, keeps Fan from being raped. The narrators are careful to emphasize that although Fan had been frightened, "otherwise she was unsullied" (197). The word "unsullied" reasserts that Fan has not been raped but also stresses her purity. Despite her pregnancy, something presented as the result of curiosity, she remains untouched—nearly virginal. Even while constantly facing extreme dangers, our heroine remains above the indignities and assaults of a cruel world.

Fan's exceptionalism is highlighted when she meets the missing girls who had come before her. Unlike her predecessors, she has been rescued from sexual assault by Miss Cathy, but Fan too becomes a captive pet to her rescuer. Coddled and spoiled by Miss Cathy after the assault, Fan soon joins the seven other girls who live in Miss Cathy's wing of the mansion. All seven of the earlier girls had been taken to live with Miss Cathy after Mister Leo had tired of them. Some had grown into adulthood in captivity but in a state of arrested development. Traumatized by their experience with Mister Leo, the girls feel love and gratitude toward Miss Cathy, a form of Stockholm syndrome. Each girl has abandoned her name, taking a number from One through Seven. In another attempt to obliterate reality and lose themselves in self-negating fantasy, each girl has had her eyes surgically altered to resemble anime-style drawings so that "their bizarrely large eyes made them look deeply attentive, like some puppy or dog who craves only your company and succor" but also "as if they were all quietly longing for someone or something, that they would always be searching" (212–13).[23]

The girls fill their days by drawing autobiographical murals with markers, a medium that reinforces their childlike state.[24] Drawing in anime style on the wall, they depict their different life stories, and yet all share the same plot of losing their true families, their abuse from Mister Leo, and their joining the group of girls. When they depict their abuse, they superimpose Mister Leo's face over their own. Because they live confined, routine lives, the remaining murals are filled with fantasy manga. Each girl dreams of an alternative life for herself and depicts it in real and convincing detail. Storytelling in this scene is multivalent. The practice of this art sustains the girls in their captivity and gives them purpose while they maintain some semblance of identity in the recording of their stories. Yet this same art form placates them and leaves them trapped; the mural has more vibrancy and reality than their actual real-life existences do.

Fan poses for inclusion in the mural, but from the start she is different from the rest. Although she replies when called Eight, the girls call her by her true name; through Fan's example of independent identity, the narrators posit that it is Fan who leads the girls to stop drawing Mister Leo in place of themselves. Fan realizes that the girls cannot simply be set free given their fragile mental health; yet when she tells them her story of searching for Reg, they endeavor to make her story real. The narrators reflect that "the funny thing about the tale of Fan is that much of what happened to her happened to her" (227). Although it is emphasized that Fan "showed plenty of her own volition," most of what happens in the novel is the result of Fan acclimating to her new environment and staying above the fray until a new opportunity arises. Only when the girls make themselves deathly ill in an effort to provide Fan with an escape does Fan break free of the gilded prison. Unable to take actions on their own behalf, the girls instead put all of their hopes on the success of Fan, much as the other writers of this story, the collective narrators of B-Mor, do.

After her escape, Fan ends up living with Vikram Upendra, a Charter doctor embroiled in a love affair with his best friend's wife, Betty Cheung. Here the novel moves from surrealistic dystopia to the familiar suburban problems of Lee's earlier novels. The novel becomes a rumination on the contrast between material success and the emotional vacancy of the wealthy and upper middle class. The wealth of the Charters seems obscene when compared to the poverty and desperation of life in the Smokes and even in B-Mor. Yet the narration remains sympathetic to the emotional lives of these privileged characters. Even the iciest Charter character, Vik's cuckolded friend Oliver, becomes a more complex character when it is revealed—in a turn requiring mythic levels of suspension of disbelief—that he is Fan's long-lost brother Liwei.

Liwei is legendary in his own right in B-Mor as one of the few residents who scored so exceptionally high on school examinations that he was permitted to join a Charter village. Like an extreme version of the SAT, these exams let a tiny percentage of those from lower social classes advance into Charter life. This advancement is so rare in B-Mor that no one concerns himself or herself with preparation. For those in the Charters, the stakes are much higher, as the lowest scoring students are "slated for service jobs such as retail or teaching or firefighting, unless, of course, they inherit enough money to make a sizable contribution to the directorate as well as permanently sustain a Charter life" (158). Lee's description of contemporary higher education all but drops the facade of being quasi-futuristic; as in the contemporary United States, class ultimately determines one's educational and occupational future. In interviews Lee has acknowledged the connection between the novel's critique of class immobility and the state of contemporary American life: "I fear that imbalance is becoming a chronic condition of our life now, in America and elsewhere. Let's be honest—I think we can all sense how drastic the differences are between the Haves and the Have Nots. Or there's a third demographic now, the Have Alls. And you don't need to be an economist to know it's not just about wealth, to know that to a great extent wealth governs what kind of education one receives, what kind of health care one can expect. And that these in turn determine the possibilities for opportunity and mobility, which everyone agrees is vital, and is the way one bridges those differences."[25] Lee's interest in this book, then, is to explore the changes, both cultural and moral, that happen when class mobility is no longer a plausible reality.

Because attaining great heights is largely unimaginable, B-Mor celebrates its successful children with parties and monuments, but they never expect to see those chosen children again. Success means severing connections to home, as this educational upward mobility is meant to be one-directional. Even though the vast majority will never have these opportunities, the possibilities present for this chosen percentage placate the higher hopes and dreams of the community and resign them to their own limited options. The narrators note, "You just see that he's traveled to a kind of heaven, if that's in your belief system, a place that is presumably better in every way than it is here, and surely never worse" (160). The fantasy for the few serves as a safety valve for the many—so much so that when the percentage of B-Mor children who pass the exam is reduced further, the uprising of B-Mor begins. The narrators describe the qualifying exam as "a lottery, aptitude based, of course, but a lottery nonetheless, and therefore [it] functions primarily in the realm of imagination and dreams" (296). If the artifice of this lottery is fully exposed, then the hopelessness of the majority cannot help but be exposed as well.

Fan's eldest brother has won this lottery. At first meeting, Liwei, now calling himself Oliver,[26] has achieved a level of financial and professional success unrivaled even among the elite. A scientist working for the C-industry, Oliver creates a drug called "Asimil"—whose name applies as much to Oliver's "assimilation" to Charter culture as it does to the drug itself—that could potentially provide continuing therapy to those who have stopped responding to the many C-drug therapies. Because Asimil would keep the C-industry profitable, Oliver has sold his patent for a fortune. His friend Vik has resisted this profitable but morally suspect research, arguing that survival rates from C-illness had not dramatically lengthened life spans in over a hundred years while the barrage of therapies kept people in a constant state of illness (277).[27] Determined to achieve unrivaled corporate and financial success to validate his assimilation to the dominant class, Oliver does not similarly question the morality of his creation; maintaining his position at the highest rungs of the elite is his sole concern.

Despite his success—or perhaps because of the struggles he faced in becoming a success—Oliver is emotionally detached from his family and nostalgically longs for the life he left behind in B-Mor. Hoping to recapture the communal living of his childhood, Oliver uses his new fortune to begin building a replica of a B-Mor street. Using his memories to create a romanticized, sanitized version of B-Mor, Oliver, now insisting on being called by his birth name, wants to create a space of "intimacy naturally elaborated enough to encompass every moment of their days, which frankly, none of them had been experiencing much, if at all, and would have gone on missing if this great fortune had not come" (106). Liwei's ironic commitment to re-creating the intimacy of B-Mor living leads to his interest in Fan. Although he left B-Mor before her birth, Fan is his only family link to B-Mor. Fan becomes a fetish for her brother in his attempt to recapture "authentic" B-Mor community feeling.

As with the ill-advised acquisitiveness of Jack Battle in *Aloft,* Oliver and his wife are "relentlessly pushing as if they were trying to overcome a huge deficit, despite how far they were already ahead" (310). Continually trying to fill an emotional void materially, the Cheungs are, of course, doomed to failure. When he discovers that his wife is having an affair with his best friend, the morally complex Vik, Oliver, like Jerry Battle in his tennis match with Rita's new boyfriend, responds in a macho sports competition that is ostensibly over a woman but is as much about ego. After their swimming competition ends in a fistfight, their friendship is over, but Oliver's marriage continues without emotional resolution.

Oliver is deeply in debt due to the building of the new B-Mor; his contract has not been signed and his credit is frozen. On the cusp of financial ruin (and thus exile from his Charter life), Oliver agrees to exchange the pregnant Fan for a final signature on his Asimil contract. Oliver's drug, along with all other existing pharmaceuticals, is obsolete in the face of the alternative that a C-free Reg presents. Fan's unborn child, like Reg, is likewise of research interest to a corporation dependent on the sale of C-drugs. Oliver betrays his only remaining family to sell Asimil, revealing just how little the success of an exceptional individual does for the family—and community—left behind.

The novel ends with Fan disappearing on the road, having been saved by Betty and Vik from Oliver's plan. Alone and pregnant, Fan continues on her journey to find Reg. The narrators and other historians of the legend of Fan lose track of her at this point but conclude with a direct address to their heroine: "You need not come back for us" (352). These lines echo the sentiment of June Han's brother Ji-Young in *The Surrendered* when he releases her from familial responsibility and sends her forward to reconstruct her life during the war. After the narrative has constructed Fan as the embodiment of B-Mor's hope for a better future, this address underscores Fan's freedom, so that while the narrators are ostensibly giving her permission to continue her life unfettered by her community, it is reaffirmed that Fan has already taken this freedom for herself upon leaving.

These final lines bring the novel full circle, back to the epigrams from Shakespeare and the band Journey that open the story. In *Julius Caesar,* Brutus beseeches Cassius to "take the current when it serves / Or lose our ventures." An exhortation to seize opportunity when it arises and take risks for greater glory, this passage contrasts Fan's free will and willingness to take chances with those of B-Mor whose lives are "bound in shallows and in miseries."[28] In using the lyrics from "Only the Young," Lee stresses the generational divide between the young and the old, as "Only the young can say / They're free to fly away." The significance of Fan's journey is in the appeal of her form of freedom, a freedom that is fully beyond the imagination of a society whose main characteristic is its routinized stagnation. The story of Fan begins as a question: Why did she leave? The story concludes with little understanding but a persistence of hope.

While in *On Such a Full Sea* Lee seems to address the lack the political critique that some critics identified in his earlier work, he interestingly uses the same characterization mechanism (the projection of male/community desires onto the blank canvas of a female figure) to carry out the project. The stories about Fan told in B-Mor, and in fact the story we are reading, are really more about the B-Mor community than about Fan herself, a point Lee makes repeatedly throughout the novel: "We have previously indicated that Fan had larger aims in leaving B-Mor, but perhaps this is not necessarily true. It may be more a matter of our own shifting perspective on that brief period, what we have come to overlay upon her journeys as we revisit them over time than anything she herself was conceiving, planning, implementing. . . . We won't say 'convictions,' because it is not in the least clear that she was marching for some cause or platform. And though it seems impossible to think this now, she may not have had any of us in mind, at any juncture" (156). The narrators overlay political resistance on a person whom they are unable to consult, who has left no record of any sort of "conviction" or cause. The narrators question their own reliability, noting defensively that "our elaborations [are] not fantastical or untrue but at times [are] vulnerable to our wishes for her, and for ourselves" (33). While Fan as a figure is real, they insist, any significance of her story is a complete construction, one that worries the narrators throughout the novel.

Fan is a bizarrely antiheroic heroine with no action, philosophy, or direction propelling her forward. Fan, as a character, is an enigma. She is described in abstract terms, reflecting back values that the narrators deem special. This is brilliantly reflected in the cover design of the hardcover edition: Fan has no face.[29] Fan serves as an embodiment of the narrators' hopes and ideals. They admit to not knowing Fan's thoughts and feelings while simultaneously celebrating her "character, which never wavered through her many trials," her moral constancy, and her "integrity" (152). They acknowledge that she is not "especially charismatic, or visionary, or subtly, cleverly aggressive in insinuating an agenda to the larger imagination" but praise her for showing "her own volition" (227). This independence and volition, it turns out, are the keys to B-Mor's preoccupation with Fan; she, unlike the rest of the herdlike community, breaks free of the expected path for citizens there: "She was as free as she had believed, and always had been. Only in leaving was it confirmed" (338).

This is what motivates the interest in Fan—she left and showed independence of vision.[30] This alone causes her character to reflect the projected wish for freedom that the others' predetermined, laboring lives curtail.

As the economy of B-Mor's community is threatened by a decreased demand from the Charter communities for the fish they raise, the tight cultural cohesion that unifies B-Mor unravels. The story of Fan is translated into street art, with representations of Fan and her lover becoming emblematic of discontent; the narrators note, "A legend can be made . . . one crude stroke at a time" (15). In an interview with David Naimon, Lee noted that Fan is "almost more of a mirror in terms of how they're looking out at the world": "they find her captivating because of her bravery, which is a bravery of 'being there' rather than saying or doing something so brave; and they also see how her departure has left a void in their lives. It allows them to begin analyzing that void in all the ways that it's unsatisfactory."[31] Fan, then, becomes the symbol for a more socially and economically equal society.

However, as Chuh noted in her treatment of *A Gesture Life,* "The consequences of the mythification of both nation and woman consequent to this trope are obvious: erasure of complexity and contradiction, the ascription of a fictive unity/purity that cannot and does not exist, and particularly with the category 'woman,' the effective undermining of an ability to have standing as a person."[32] The depiction of Fan as the object of B-Mor's mythology, like Hata's mythification of K, creates a one-dimensional character without a knowable depth or personality. While Fan is constructed by the B-Mor narrators to be the ideal liberal subject, it is her mythification that reiterates time and again that the story of Fan is a fantasy project, as their dystopian world is founded on unfettered neoliberalism that creates and upholds the racialized colonization of B-Mor.

The use of Fan as a symbol for liberal ideas in *On Such a Full Sea* is particularly intriguing when this character is compared to another unknowable woman from Lee's earliest work, *Native Speaker.* The critic Juliana Chang, in discussing Lee's debut novel, noted that the narrator's Korean housekeeper, called only Ahjuma—or the Korean equivalent to "Ma'am"—is the only character in the novel "who remains opaque" and "outside human connection, identification, or sympathy."[33] Yet this unintelligibility of character, according to Chang, plays a valuable role in the novel: "Ahjuma blocks the fantasy of liberal universal humanism that undergirds the romance of American democracy, citizenship, and exceptionalism."[34] Chang viewed the abject characterization of Ahjuma as putting a valuable check on a novel that otherwise seems to allegorize the neoliberal shift from public sphere to private sphere—the only place in the novel that allows for the narrator's "self-actualization." It is Ahjuma's very unknowability that refuses attempts to assimilate her and place her in the dominant world order.

Despite the similarity in opaque presentation by unreliable narrators, Fan is not an abject figure; where Ahjuma shows no real agency, Fan does. In contrast, Fan is the dream of American individualism—she both breaks away from her communal-minded kin to set out on her voyage and refuses to assimilate to the culture of the elite. Her motivations and internal integrity are her own, and while she rarely interferes in the lives of others, neither does she lose her sense of self. Unfortunately, the reader has no sense of who that self is or what motivates her. Fan, like Ahjuma, is "a cipher" and still filtered through another's consciousness, but Fan—for all her impenetrability—is an individual. Whereas Ahjuma "blocks the fantasy of liberal universal humanism," Fan is the fantasy of liberal universal humanism. She is the lone imagined holdout in a world that has given up on freedom.

The story ends not in Fan's reunion with her lost love or the successful overthrow of oppressive structures, but in the slow deflation of the conventions of the girl-hero archetype. The novel is filled with genre refusals: rather than feature one catastrophic apocalyptic event, we have a world reordered based on slow environmental collapse and human exploitation; the heroine is decidedly unheroic in action; and the revolution she inspires fades into nothing but a legend of what might have been. Lee self-consciously creates a heroine who is intentionally unlike the heroine of our expectations and calls our attention to this contrast throughout the novel.[35] The communal narrator repeatedly celebrates her difference: "The more we follow the turns of her journey, the more we realize that she is not quite the champion we would normally sing; she is not the heroine who wields the great sword; she is not the bearer of wisdom and light; she does not head the growing column, leading a new march. She is one of the ranks, this perfectly ordinary, exquisitely tiny person in whom we will reside, via both living and dreaming" (198). At another point in the text, when Fan has the opportunity to harm a woman who has been keeping Fan and a half dozen other young women prisoners, the narrators note, "Another sort of heroine might have summoned the darkest parts of herself, resolving, by either bestial fury or righteous mantle, to wield. . . . Of course, she did not" (245–46). The heroine celebrated by B-Mor shows quiet heroism, a heroism that demands respect and does not rely on violent, aggressive forms of power.[36]

Fan's very lack of heroic characteristics forces readers to confront their own expectations about what makes a heroine. While in the elite Charter villages, Fan watches an action movie about a "girl counter-cyberterrorism agent" and has an emotional reaction to the film: "by the end, after the heroine is physically destroyed but rises again, whole in form but entirely changed, Fan felt a sudden hollowing in her chest, a flash cavern of longing that she had not yet known" (261). The plucky dystopian heroine, Lee suggests, feeds a reader's or a viewer's psychic need for rebellion or change, causing an indistinct sense of longing. Yet this experience, like that of the novel, is a version of consumerist fantasy—one that requires no action, reimagined philosophy, or danger. In wanting Fan to do more, to be more like the girl "counter-cyberterrorism agent," to be more like Katniss Everdeen, we as readers, like the narrators of B-Mor, are also projecting our desires for a better self. Yet we might conclude, as the narrators do, that a girl cannot be "prophetic [or] chosen, at last, to lead anyone but herself" (348).

The legend of Fan is a story, a construction. The fictive nature of Fan could undercut the novel's hope for or belief in a truly free individual. The failure of the B-Mor resistance movement, inspired by Fan's legend, then, might be inevitable because all they really have is an idealized story of true individual freedom—an amorphous hope that there is an escape from the rigid social and economic structures by which everyone is bound. The economy of B-Mor recovers slightly, and like Occupy Wall Street, the resistance fades.[37] The narrators lament the passing of the "disturbance," reporting that it is as if they all "just slept through" the key moment.

Yet a small number who remember the story remain: "some of us, like spies in a perilous land, will meet a certain gaze; and once we do, that recognition can soften the most wary eye and make us want to exchange all kinds of notations again, even the more improbable tales and rumors, to report everything we know of our Fan" (338). What remains is the memory of the moment, the old stories of Fan and B-Mor's lost potential. The story is what matters most and what carries the most subversive potential. Lee has argued that his novel stresses art as an "almost political idea": "[The novel is] an assertion that we only become individuals when we have that creative urge. We are not just consumers; we are not just surviving. That's our gift as humans. It's not just about survival. It's not just about being comfortable. The book is worried that all those things are now perfectly acceptable definitions of being human and says, 'No, they're not.' And Fan is the only thing that really inspires that kind of urge, that urge for a different kind of creation."[38] In creating the story, then, the people of B-Mor have found a way back into their humanity, and its potential remains latent even at the end of the book.

On Such a Full Sea, like all of the novels in Lee's canon, explores the many paradoxes of storytelling. Finding a voice through a story allows even the most alienated characters to engage with the world and reckon with the emotional truths they have suppressed and misrepresented. From Henry Park's struggle to find an honest voice in *Native Speaker* to Doc Hata's long-overdue confession of his own guilt in *A Gesture Life,* and from Jerry Battle's recognition of his responsibilities to his family in *Aloft* to June Han's and Hector Brennan's reconciliation with the traumas of their pasts in *The Surrendered,* Lee explores the way people use stories to make meaning—and to hide from it. His body of work examines the stories we tell to hide from our loved ones, our histories, our responsibilities, and above all, ourselves. But in the telling of these stories we are also able to acknowledge the truth of our lives, providing an opportunity for change and transformation if we are brave enough to "take the current when it serves."

NOTES

Chapter 1—Understanding Chang-rae Lee

1. Charles McGrath, "Deep in Suburbia," *New York Times,* February 29, 2004.

2. Boris Kachka, "Pigging Out with Writers Gary Shteyngart and Chang-rae Lee," *Vulture,* January 7, 2014.

3. Dwight Garner, "An Interview: Adopted Voice," *New York Times,* September 5, 1999.

4. Lee described this first effort as "a big, ambitious, crazy novel about a cult in NYC based around a psychotropic mushroom that 'played' a fixed 'show' in all who ingested it; it was inspired by Pynchon and DeLillo and was very consciously superliterary and also pretty awful." See David Naimon, "A Conversation with Chang-rae Lee," *Missouri Review* 37.1 (Spring 2014): 122.

5. Kachka, "Pigging Out."

6. For a discussion of the marketing of the book, see Wu, "Native Sons and Native Speakers."

7. Pam Belluck, "Being of Two Cultures and Belonging to Neither: After an Acclaimed Novel, a Korean-American Writer Searches for His Roots," *New York Times,* July 10, 1995.

8. Rand Richards Cooper, "Excess Identities," *New York Times,* April 9, 1995.

9. When Lee was asked to name a work of "immigrant fiction" that influenced him, he selected Carlos Bulosan's *America Is in the Heart* (1946). Though it is a "somewhat sentimental novel and full of really searing scenes about injustice and racism," Lee experienced the work as "deeply emotional and satisfying." See Naimon, "A Conversation," 132.

10. Yoonmee Chang, "Ethnic Entrepreneurs," 66.

11. David Palumbo-Liu, *Asian/American: Historical Crossings of a Racial Frontier* (Stanford, Calif.: Stanford University Press, 1999), 396.

12. Chuh, *Imagine Otherwise,* 16.

13. Ibid., 18.

14. Christine Lee Zilka, "Interview with Chang-rae Lee," *Kartika Review* 6 (Fall/Winter 2009).

15. Ibid. Zilka referenced another *Kartika* interview with the writer Don Lee, in which he commended Chang-rae Lee for being "brave" enough to have a white narrator for *Aloft* and thus "starting a mini-revolution" for Asian American writers. Chang-rae Lee, however, downplayed the negative response to *Aloft,* but he did comment on Asian American gatekeeping and concluded that he did not want to be read "solely because of the subject matter of 'ethnicity' of my books."

16. Bruce Fulton, "The Drama of Identity: A Conversation with Chang-rae Lee," *Koreana* 10.2 (Summer 1996). Accessed July 25, 2016. http://www.koreana.or.kr/.

17. Sarah Anne Johnson, "Chang-rae Lee: The Drama of Consciousness," in *The Very Telling: Conversations with American Writers* (Lebanon, N.H.: University Press of New England, 2006), 110.

18. Huang, "Chang-rae Lee and the Counter-Gestures of Life Writing," 30.

19. Sedlmeier, "Rereading Literary Form," 221.

20. Michelle Young-Mee Rhee, "Greater Lore," 172.

21. Garner, "An Interview."

22. In a later counterpart to "Coming Home Again," "Eat, Memory" (2004), Lee wrote of his life in New York City in 1990 as his mother was dying upstate. In this brief piece he recounted how moving he found the film *Babette's Feast* at a time when he was trying to become an artist and using food to express his grief over his mother's declining health.

23. Hurst, "Balancing Self and Other through Speech and Silence in Chang-rae Lee's *Native Speaker* and Amy Tan's *The Hundred Secret Senses*," 88. Several books have been written about the significance of food in Asian American literature. See Wenying Xu, *Eating Identities: Reading Food in Asian American Literature* (Honolulu: University of Hawaii Press, 2008); and Jennifer Ann Ho, *Consumption and Identity in Asian American Coming-of-Age Novels* (New York: Routledge, 2005).

24. McGrath, "Deep in Suburbia."

25. Lee has been quoted in several articles suggesting that Jerry Battle was inspired by his actual Italian American father-in-law and Lee's own suburban experience. See Johnson, *The Very Telling*, 117; and Lorna Bradbury, "Chang-rae Lee: Lorna Bradbury Meets a Korean-American Novelist Who's Obsessed with the Suburbs," *Telegraph*, June 20, 2004.

26. Lee dedicated *A Gesture Life* to Hong.

27. Fulton, "The Drama of Identity."

28. "Chang-rae Lee: By the Book," *New York Times Sunday Book Review*, January 23, 2014.

29. Belluck, "Being of Two Cultures and Belonging to Neither."

Chapter 2—"A life univocal"

1. Song, "A Diasporic Future," 80.

2. Wu, "Native Sons and Native Speakers." Wu noted that *Native Speaker* was removed from contention as a 2002 selected reading for New York City when a group of Korean Americans protested its inclusion on the basis of perpetuating stereotypes of "Asian inscrutability by casting Park as a spy" (1460). Jane Yoo similarly argued that Lee "depicts an incomplete and distorted portrayal of Korean American lives" by suggesting that Korean Americans "can all be characterized as traitors to our roots" ("Cultural Alienation and the Asian American: Chang-rae Lee, *Native Speaker*," *Asian American Policy Review* 14 [2005]: 59).

3. Patricia Chu, *Assimilating Asians: Gendered Strategies of Authorship in Asian America* (Durham, N.C.: Duke University Press, 2000), 3.

4. Cowart, "Korean Connection," 119.

5. Xiang, "The Korean Voice of American Empire," 295.

6. Corley, "Just Another Ethnic Pol," 62.

7. Arac, "Violence and the Human Voice," 61.

8. In her influential book *Immigrant Acts: On Asian American Cultural Politics* (Durham, N.C.: Duke University Press, 1996), Lisa Lowe explained the relationship between Asian stereotypes and the construction of who qualifies for citizenship in U.S. history: "In the last century and a half, the American *citizen* has been defined over against the Asian immigrant, legally, economically, and culturally. These definitions have cast Asian immigrants both as persons and as populations to be integrated into the national political sphere and as the contradictory, confusing, unintelligible, elements to be marginalized and returned to their alien origins. 'Asia' has been always a complex site on which the manifold anxieties of the U.S. nation-state have been figured: such anxieties have figured Asian countries as exotic, barbaric, and alien, and Asian laborers immigrating to the United States from the nineteenth century onward as a 'yellow peril' threatening to displace white European immigrants" (4).

9. Chen, "Impersonation and Other Disappearing Acts," 640.

10. Parikh, "Ethnic America Undercover," 275.

11. Ludwig, "Ethnicity as Cognitive Identity." Ludwig argued that the novel ultimately moves away from the significance of bodies to stress speech as the basis of identity (223); this, she concluded, has more potential to unify people regardless of ethnic or cultural background (234).

12. See Engles, "Visions of Me in the Whitest Raw Light," for a larger discussion of how Henry filters his perceptions of the world through "a middle-class white perspective" (28).

13. In "Korean Connection," Cowart noted that Shelley's poem "features a famous affirmation of ethnicity transcended. . . . Its author imagines the self's prospective deliverance in terms that might under different circumstances, inspire or comfort a student chained to the rock of grade-school pedagogy and suffering, Prometheus-like, the contumely of a classroom despot" (117). Lee's choice of this difficult but rebellious poem underscores that it is not the language that tortures the young immigrant but the use of it as a weapon to exclude that harms Henry.

14. In *Sexual Naturalization: Asian Americans and Miscegenation* (Stanford, Calif.: Stanford University Press, 2004), Susan Koshy wrote that in the early twentieth century marriages between white American women and foreigners could result in loss of the wives' American citizenship through the Expatriation Act of 1907. This law was amended by the Cable Act of 1922, which "struck down the principle of derivative citizenship, except in cases where the women had married 'aliens ineligible to citizenship,' which is how Asians were classified. Hence, white women who crossed the color line to marry were selectively denationalized" (7). While Henry's marriage to Lelia serves to provide evidence of his full assimilation, historically marriage worked against interracial couples (in this gender configuration) to the extreme of an American woman's loss of citizenship.

15. The experience of Henry's father in *Native Speaker* is reminiscent of Lee's "Uncle Chul Gets Rich" from his 1996 *New York Times Magazine* story. Like Mr. Park, Lee's no-account uncle opened a store in a rough neighborhood in the Bronx with ten thousand dollars borrowed from Lee's father. Lee explained that though the area was high risk, Chul had no competition; the racial dynamics of Korean-owned businesses in downtrodden urban areas touched on in this essay are a central issue in his novel. Although Uncle Chul eventually struck it rich, he lost touch with his family and lived a stressful life.

16. In his subsequent novels *A Gesture Life* and *Aloft*, Lee more fully explores the experience of being a minority in a white suburb. Like Henry's father, *A Gesture Life*'s Doc Hata's economic success does not facilitate genuine connection with most of his neighbors. *Aloft*'s Daisy Battle is so isolated that her depression goes unchecked while she is living the American dream. The familiar trope of suburban alienation gains deeper resonance when applied to recent immigrant subjects.

In *America's Asia: Racial Form and American Literature, 1893–1945* (Princeton, N.J.: Princeton University Press, 2005), Colleen Lye traced the history of the function of Asian American stereotypes in preventing genuine class analysis: "Until the birth of Buck's and Steinbeck's model economic characters, the Asiatic figures of early-twentieth-century American literature (despot, coolie, mask) referred not to persons but to a host of modernity's dehumanizing effects (laboring conditions, group entities, corporations). Yet these figures were the also [*sic*] ancestors of today's stereotypical Asian American. The initial textual presence of Asiatic racial form as an economic trope helps to explain the primarily economic themes of Asian American racial representation. That a genealogy of Asian American stereotype is discernable in the historical failures of class critique, in the end, I hope, helps shed some light on the painful historical divorce between the homely longings of Asian immigrants and the utopian aspirations of actually existing American liberal reform movements, from Progressivism to affirmation action" (11).

17. In contrast to the critics who saw the novel as fictionalized autobiography, Lee, unlike Henry Park, chose not to take an "American" name when starting school. See chapter 1 for discussion of Lee's decision to keep his given name.

18. Physical spaces are used as metaphors throughout the novel for the culturally inflected ways people interact with each other. Lelia, for example, feels more "safe" in her father-in-law's home than in her childhood home (216). At the conclusion of the novel, Henry and his wife return to their loft apartment that is filled with open space and few walls to divide them.

19. The inadequacy of replicating food memories was the focus of Lee's essay "Coming Home Again," as discussed in chapter 1, when Lee tried to cook his mother's dishes to please himself and his father in the wake of his mother's death. In *Native Speaker* the distance between father and son after Henry's mother's death is evident in their meals together, which they eat "without savor" while hiding their emotions from each other (59). By contrast, the health of Henry's marriage can be evaluated by the frequency of shared meals, meals that are integrated with sex.

20. Park and Wald, "Native Daughters in the Promised Land," 622. Wu cited Trudier Harris's critique of *Native Son* and Wald and Park's of *Native Speaker* to argue that these feminist critics were reductively "holding out for more responsible representations" that demand an impossible authenticity. He argued instead, "Invested in their protagonists, the novels may speak only indirectly, if at all, to the textual deployment of femininity as the material ground for ethnicity. But that ground cannot be avoided in their juxtaposition" (Wu, "Native Sons and Native Speakers," 1472.).

21. Park and Wald, "Native Daughters in the Promised Land," 609.

22. See chapter 1 for discussion of Lee's mother's poor acculturation upon moving to the United States.

23. Cowart, "Korean Connection," 118.

24. Caton, "A Korean American Perspective," 126.

25. Ludwig, "Ethnicity as Cognitive Identity," 237.

26. Cowart, "Korean Connection," 125.

27. Jodi Kim, "From Mee-Gook to Gook," 252.

28. Chen, "Impersonation and Other Disappearing Acts," 642.

29. Parikh, "Ethnic America Undercover," 251.

30. Michelle Young-Mee Rhee, "Greater Lore," 159.

31. Chen, "Impersonation and Other Disappearing Acts," 638.

32. Narkunas, "Surfing the Long Waves of Global Capital," 348.

33. Min Hyoung Song argued that Luzan's pro-Marcos fund-raising in the United States makes this sort of collective solidarity "suspect" since it would be counter to U.S. foreign policy; Henry's role in Luzan's downfall is part of the "need to be disciplined" (Song, "A Diasporic Future," 87).

34. Chen, "Impersonation and Other Disappearing Acts," 639.

35. Parikh, "Ethnic America Undercover," 273.

36. Jirousek, "A New Book of the Land," 14.

37. Mae M. Ngai, *Impossible Subjects: Illegal Aliens and the Making of Modern America* (Princeton, N.J.: Princeton University Press, 2004), 238.

38. Ibid., 262.

39. Ngai complicated this seemingly progressive trajectory toward equality in immigration law, however, to discuss how the Immigration Act of 1965 opened the doors to Asian and African immigrants; immigration was ultimately more restricted for those coming from the Western hemisphere (ibid., 263).

40. Ludwig saw Kwang as reminiscent of John F. Kennedy, whose moral political persona did not correspond to his behavior in his personal life (Ludwig, "Ethnicity as Cognitive Identity," 228). Betsey Huang compared Kwang to Barack Obama for his use of the "politics of inclusion" a decade before Obama became a senator (Huang, "Citizen Kwang," 247).

41. Huang, "Citizen Kwang," 248.

42. Ibid., 249.

43. Park and Wald, "Native Daughters in the Promised Land," 629.

44. For an extended exploration of the idea of "racial triangulation" that included the "relative valorization" of one group as compared to another in service to another, more dominant group, see Claire Jean Kim, "The Racial Triangulation of Asian Americans," *Politics & Society* 27 (March 1999): 105–38. For more discussion of how Lee uses triangulation in the novel, see James Kyung-Jin Lee, "Where the Talented Tenth Meets the Model Minority."

45. Daniel Y. Kim, "Do I, Too, Sing America." Kim read Kwang as Lee's creative invention to fill in the real-life lack of Korean American representatives amid incidents of racial conflict in the 1990s (237).

46. Kun Jong Lee, "Towards Interracial Understanding and Identification." This author also noted that in his depictions of the boycotts, "Lee seems to compress the fifteen-year history of black-led boycotts of Korean American stores in [New York City] from 1981 to 1995 into one year" (754).

47. Ibid., 755.

48. Claire Jean Kim, *Bitter Fruit: The Politics of Black-Korean Conflict in New York City* (New Haven, Conn.: Yale University Press, 2000), 2.

49. Corley saw Lee invoking the Dutch history of New York City in Mayor De Roos's name and providing a sly commentary on the "permanence of ethnic difference and they dynamic of assimilation that hides the social, economic, and political value accruing to

whiteness" ("Just Another Ethnic Pol," 67). Rachel C. Lee, "Reading Contests and Contesting Reading," picked up on Corley's suggestion and made explicit the connection between the mayor's Dutch name and "'de ruse' behind nativist political and cultural platforms that fail to assert the sovereignty of tribal nations and stoke a selective anti-immigrant sentiment" (350).

50. David Palumbo-Liu, *Asian/American: Historical Crossings of a Racial Frontier* (Stanford, Calif.: Stanford University Press, 1999), 186.

51. Kun Jong Lee, "Towards Interracial Understanding and Identification," 756.

52. Lowe, *Immigrant Acts*, 35.

53. Corley, "Just Another Ethnic Pol," 74.

54. Cowart, "Korean Connection," 116–17.

55. Arac, "Violence and the Human Voice," 62.

56. Daniel Y. Kim, "Do I, Too, Sing America," 235.

57. Daniel Y. Kim also pointed out the ways in which reviews highlighted *Invisible Man* in relationship to the novel, which minimized *Native Speaker* to an "act of authorial impersonation" that turned Henry into "an invisible man in yellowface, a spook of another color" (ibid., 231).

58. Ibid., 233.

59. Chen, "Impersonation and Other Disappearing Acts," 654.

60. Moraru, "Speakers and Sleepers," 79.

61. Wu, "Native Sons and Native Speakers," 10.

62. Rody, "With Darkness Yet," 77.

63. Daniel Y. Kim, "Do I, Too, Sing America," 235.

64. Ibid., 74.

65. Ibid., 78.

66. Hurst, "Balancing Self and Other," connected Lee's use of "lurk" to his naming of a minor character, Chillingsworth, to suggest a connection between Nathaniel Hawthorne's *The Scarlet Letter* and *Native Speaker* (86).

67. Cowart, "Korean Connection," 119.

68. Ibid., 120.

69. See Ludwig, "Ethnicity as Cognitive Identity," 228, for more on the significance of the Kennedys to the novel.

70. Yoonmee Chang, "Ethnic Entrepreneurs," 137.

71. Cowart, "Korean Connection," 121.

72. Arac, "Violence and the Human Voice," 65.

73. The critic Lou Freitas Caton found hope for forgiveness in Henry's efforts at confession ("A Korean American Perspective," 122).

74. Narkunas, "Surfing the Long Waves of Global Capital," 348.

75. Song, "A Diasporic Future," 92.

76. Rody, "With Darkness Yet," 66.

77. Moraru, "Speakers and Sleepers," 70.

78. Parikh, "Ethnic America Undercover," 260.

79. Huang, "Citizen Kwang," 250.

80. Chen, "Impersonation and Other Disappearing Acts," 660. Lori Jirousek disagreed with Chen's interpretation of the ending to suggest that Henry does make a positive change, one that embodies a more inclusive sense of himself that echoes Gloria Anzaldua's idea of "new tribalism" in which identifications cross all usual boundaries (Jirousek, "A New Book of the Land," 20).

81. Cowart, "Korean Connection," 125.

82. Song, "A Diasporic Future," 96; Jodi Kim, "From Mee-Gook to Gook," 134. Song further argued that Henry becomes like one of the marginalized Korean women who Park and Wald argue serve as "legitimation of a male immigrant subject in the public sphere" ("A Diasporic Future," 609) when his life in the public sphere collapses (ibid., 96).

83. Ludwig, "Ethnicity as Cognitive Identity," 239.

84. Parikh, "Ethnic America Undercover," 281.

85. Tsou, "This Doesn't Mean What You'll Think," 585.

86. Ibid.

87. Parikh, "Ethnic America Undercover," 281.

88. Moraru, "Speakers and Sleepers," 89. Moraru saw this "Whitmanesque heterogeneity" as a means of breaking down white privilege: "In Lelia, the native at last speaks in tongues. Le(e)lia finally earns her nickname, 'Lee.' Thus, it is she, rather than Henry, who becomes Chang-rae Lee's 'alter-alter-ego'" ("Speakers and Sleepers," 88).

89. Tsou complicated this argument further by suggesting that the negative implications of "making the sympathetic white mother the normalizing figure through which these differences must pass to be articulated" require a minimizing of the "longer history of racialization and capitalist exploitation" ("This Doesn't Mean What You'll Think," 586).

Chapter 3—"The basic mode of wartime"

1. Michiko Kakutani, "Fitting in Perfectly on the Outside, but Lost Within," review of *A Gesture Life,* by Chang-rae Lee, *New York Times,* August 31, 1999.

2. Dwight Garner, "An Interview: Adopted Voice," *New York Times*, September 5, 1999.

3. See also So-Hee Lee, "Cultural Citizenship as Subject-Making."

4. Suk Koo Rhee, "Consumable Bodies and Ethnic (Hi)Stories," 95.

5. Kong, "Beyond K's Specter," 16.

6. For historical examination of this topic, see George Hicks, *The Comfort Women: Japan's Brutal Regime of Enforced Prostitution in the Second World War* (New York: W. W. Norton, 1994); and C. Sarah Soh, *The Comfort Women: Sexual Violence and Postcolonial Memory in Korea and Japan* (Chicago: University of Chicago Press, 2009).

7. Garner, "An Interview."

8. Sarah Anne Johnson, "Chang-rae Lee: The Drama of Consciousness," in *The Very Telling: Conversations with American Writers* (Lebanon, N.H.: University Press of New England, 2006), 114.

9. Boris Kachka, "Pigging Out with Writers Gary Shteyngart and Chang-rae Lee." *Vulture*, January 7, 2014.

10. Carroll, "Traumatic Patriarchy," 593.

11. Huang, "Chang-rae Lee and the Counter-Gestures of Life Writing," 30–31.

12. Ibid., 33.

13. Ang, "The Politics of Victimization," 125.

14. Ibid., 127.

15. Dwyer, "Ethnic Home Improvement," argued that Liv Crawford's desire to buy Hata's house and her ultimate success are "an admission that passive and agreeable behavior on the part of the ethnic outsider will rarely gain him acceptance or happiness" (173).

16. Varvogli, "Chang-rae Lee, *A Gesture Life*," 104.
17. Johnson, "Chang-rae Lee," 113.
18. Suk Koo Rhee noted that Hata's racism "provides a safe opportunity to describe Korean racism while deflecting attention away from white racism"—a move that echoes the rhetoric of the L.A. riots in which white racism was lost in a media narrative of Korean-black conflict ("Consumable Bodies and Ethnic (Hi)Stories," 110).
19. Ang, "The Politics of Victimization," 134.
20. Lee's essay "The Faintest Echo of Our Language" touched on his mother's experiences of Japanese occupation in Korea. See discussion of that work in chapter 1.
21. Jerng, "Recognizing the Transracial Adoptee," 59.
22. Kong, "Beyond K's Specter," 18.
23. Suk Koo Rhee, "Consumable Bodies and Ethnic (Hi)Stories," 107.
24. Hata's paternalistic policing of Sunny's body echoes his superior officer Colonel Ishii's attitude toward the "comfort women" under his control. At one point Hata reports that Ishii speaks of the sex slaves as if they were his daughters: "'Look at my girls' . . . like a father who has been away much too long" (176). Both men cloak their domination in the pageantry of fatherhood to suggest innocent caretaking rather than the exploitation of the women they have cast as children. In both cases this paternalism resonates on a political plane as well as the personal one.
25. See Louis Allen, *Burma: The Longest War, 1941–1945* (London: Phoenix, 2000), for scholarship on the Japanese occupation of Burma. For a comparison of Lee's novel with another Asian American writer's treatment of Burma in contemporary fiction, see Chua, "Asian Americans Imagining Burma."
26. Jerng, "Recognizing the Transracial Adoptee," 55.
27. Ibid.
28. Kong, "Beyond K's Specter," 17. Motuz, "Before Speech," similarly argued that Hata's re-creation of his relationship with K in his relationship with Sunny can be viewed as a form of Freudian "repetition-compulsion" in which the subject reenacts the past without consciously knowing it. This psychological diagnosis, however, does not excuse Hata's behavior: "While this may be partly true, in a novel so careful to depict the complexities of agency, such an explanation relieves Hata of too much responsibility" (Motuz, "Before Speech," 418).
29. For a discussion of the Japanese occupation of Korea, see Jun Uchida, *Brokers of Empire: Japanese Settler Colonialism in Korea, 1876–1945* (Cambridge, Mass.: Harvard University Asia Center, Harvard University Press, 2011).
30. Jiro's sense of inferiority can be explained by the historic lack of social status of ethnic Koreans in Japan and the resulting discrimination they face. See George Hicks, *Japan's Hidden Apartheid: The Korean Minority and the Japanese* (Brookfield, Vt.: Ashgate, 1997).
31. See Kong, "Beyond K's Specter," for further application of Arendt's philosophy to the novel. Kong ultimately argued that where Arendt sees the impossibility of a moral awakening for the Nazi Adolf Eichmann, Lee does imagine that a war criminal such as Hata could find "moral absolution" (8).
32. Cheng, "Passing, Natural Selection, and Love's Failure," 561.
33. Chuh, "One Hundred Percent Korean," 109.
34. Huang, "Chang-rae Lee and the Counter-Gestures of Life Writing," 37–38.
35. Carroll, "Traumatic Patriarchy," 603.
36. Chuh, "One Hundred Percent Korean," 105.

37. Suk Koo Rhee, "Consumable Bodies and Ethnic (Hi)Stories," 96–97.

38. Lee's imagery here echoes back to a scene in *Native Speaker* when Henry first meets Lelia and pays careful attention to how she speaks: "I watched her wide full mouth sweep through her sentences like a figure touring a dark house, flipping on spots and banks of perfectly drawn light" (10–11).

39. Huang, "Chang-rae Lee and the Counter-Gestures of Life Writing," 41.

40. Cheng, "Passing, Natural Selection, and Love's Failure," 562.

41. Suk Koo Rhee, "Consumable Bodies and Ethnic (Hi)Stories," 101.

42. Cheng, "Passing, Natural Selection, and Love's Failure," 563.

43. For a compelling study of the use of "haunting" in contemporary ethnic fiction, see Kathleen Brogan, *Cultural Haunting: Ghosts and Ethnicity in Recent American Literature* (Charlottesville: University Press of Virginia, 1998).

44. Cheng, "Passing, Natural Selection, and Love's Failure," 564.

45. Carroll, "Traumatic Patriarchy," 607.

46. Christopher Lee, "Form-Giving and the Remains of Identity in *A Gesture Life*," 104.

47. Hamilton Carroll cited a passage from the novel in which Hata's desire to hide from the past echoes Whitman's "Song of Myself": "The house the darkened museum of a one-man civilization, whose latent history, if I could so will, would be left always unspoken, unsung" ("Traumatic Patriarchy," 289). This allusion to Whitman, Carroll suggested, works against the poet's "celebration of an organic, constitutive, democratic subject" (608). As in *Native Speaker,* Lee alludes to Whitman even as he complicates the democratic idealism of his predecessor.

48. Kong, "Beyond K's Specter," 19.

49. Ibid., 19–20.

50. Moraru, "The Other, the Namesake," 32. Lee plays with character names in all of his novels. Here we have Thomas, son of Lincoln, liberating Hata from his past by invoking another American hero, Franklin. The juxtaposition of the founding fathers with the failed assimilation of Jiro Kurohata reminds readers of the shortcomings of American democracy in contrast to its best ideals.

51. Dwight Garner asked Lee about the significance of his early novels being set in Westchester, New York, to which Lee replied, "Well, I grew up in Cheever country. . . . And I've always felt that Cheever country is surprisingly amenable to a man like Hata" ("An Interview").

52. Swimming pools are symbolically significant in several of Lee's novels, particularly in *Aloft* and *On Such a Full Sea*. Jerry Battle's slow reckoning with his wife's probably intentional drowning in the family pool is the central drama of *Aloft*, while *On Such a Full Sea* focuses on the journey of Fan, a professional fish-tank diver. In the latter a key scene takes place in a swimming pool as Fan's brother Oliver realizes his wife is having an affair with his best friend. While the men fight, Fan saves the family's nanny from drowning.

53. Suk Koo Rhee, "Consumable Bodies and Ethnic (Hi)Stories," 109.

54. Miller, "Chang-rae Lee's *A Gesture Life,*" 14.

55. Kong, "Beyond K's Specter," 8.

56. Although the Kono Statement of 1993, an apology for Japan's responsibility for the forced prostitution of "comfort women," was meant to put an end to denial on the part of the Japanese government of the existence of sex slavery during the war, Japanese politicians have repeatedly discounted the truth of survivors' stories. See Kong, "Beyond

K's Specter," for a discussion of the political battle in Japan over continuing denial and failure to pay reparations to most survivors.

57. Huang, "Chang-rae Lee and the Counter-Gestures of Life Writing," 45.

58. Carroll, "Traumatic Patriarchy," 611.

59. Chuh, "One Hundred Percent Korean," 107.

60. Ibid., 108.

61. Kong, "Beyond K's Specter," 2.

62. Cheng, "Passing, Natural Selection, and Love's Failure," 571.

63. Ibid., 572.

64. Young-Oak Lee in "Transcending Ethnicity Diasporicity in *A Gesture Life*" viewed the conclusion of the novel even more optimistically: "Hata's journey is that of one man unlearning colonialism, racism, patriarchy, and sexism. As he finally allows the cultural constructions to dissolve, he can ready himself for another journey which will transport him onward, and perhaps, back to the point of his origin" (78). This reading falls in line with what Belinda Kong argued is the troubling difficulty of the critical embrace of the novel: that in allowing Hata to be a person with nuance and psychological depth that are denied his victim, the novel grants Hata more humanity than it grants K ("Beyond K's Specter," 20).

Chapter 4—"The last living white man"

1. A. O. Scott, "Above It All," *New York Times Book Review,* March 14, 2004, 7.

2. Lorna Bradbury, "Chang-rae Lee: Lorna Bradbury Meets a Korean-American Novelist Who's Obsessed with the Suburbs," *Telegraph,* June 20, 2004.

3. Jerng, "Nowhere in Particular," 185.

4. Ibid., 186. Jerng further noted, "As if in anticipation of desires within the larger literary field to impose specific contexts for constructing race as meaningful, Lee disrupts conventional assignations of where and when race signifies. *Aloft* thus poses the problem of reading race when it cannot be located within modes of perception built around the literary formation of ethnic literature and ethnic author."

5. Ibid., 189–90.

6. Ibid., 194.

7. Ibid., 195.

8. Sohn, "White Flight, White Narration," 25–26.

9. Sedlmeier, "Rereading Literary Form," 213.

10. Christine Lee Zilka, "Interview with Chang-rae Lee," *Kartika Review* 6 (Fall/Winter 2009). Accessed July 25, 2016. www.kartikareview.com.

11. Sarah Anne Johnson, "Chang-rae Lee: The Drama of Consciousness," in *The Very Telling: Conversations with American Writers* (Lebanon, N.H.: University Press of New England, 2006), 117.

12. Jerng, "Nowhere in Particular," 196.

13. Sohn, "White Flight, White Narration," 39.

14. Wilhite, "Contested Terrain." Wilhite wrote, "Since the 1980s, new immigrants to the United States have been moving directly into the suburbs, remapping the history of white flight to make room for the ethnic enclave" (632). The old narrative of new immigrants crowded into impoverished urban centers, then, has been out of date for three decades, but the stories have largely stuck to this script.

15. Ibid., 637.

16. Ibid., 620.

17. Ibid., 634.

18. Knapp, "The Business of Forgetting," 209.

19. Ibid., 197.

20. Bradbury, "Chang-rae Lee."

21. Knapp, "The Business of Forgetting," 199.

22. Sohn, "White Flight, White Narration," 53.

23. Kristen Case, "Turbulence in Suburbia," *New Leader* 87 (March/April 2004): 26–27.

24. Knapp, "The Business of Forgetting," 212.

25. The tennis match in *Aloft* is echoed in *On Such a Full Sea* when the heroine's brother Oliver swims competitively with his best friend and his wife's lover. That scene, however, ends in an actual fight.

26. In response to frequent critical complaints that Jerry's narrative voice seems too academic for a middle-aged landscaper, Stephen Sohn argued that "Lee flouts mimeticism as a model for character creation, but more than that, he directs his construction to challenge stereotypical conceptions of Italian Americans" ("White Flight, White Narration," 38).

27. Sohn too saw Lee using this description of Paul Pyun's career to tease critics and readers alike: "Lee admitted, '[Paul is] someone I wrote to make fun of myself and to make fun of the image of the "Asian American writer" working out his anxieties'; Paul exists simultaneously as a 'self- critique' and as a reference to a larger discourse. . . . These 'anxieties' are perhaps related to the native-informant status of the Asian American writer, what Jerry calls 'The Problem with Being Sort of Himself,' but this rather murky predicament hinges on the phrase 'sort of,' denoting 'not fully.' Can an Asian American writer not fully be him- or herself, at least in relation to race and ethnicity? The reading practices and responses to the book suggest that this challenge still exists despite the fact that *Aloft* has been so widely and positively reviewed" ("White Flight, White Narration," 38).

28. For a discussion of Lee's autobiographical essays, see chapter 1.

29. The baby's name serves as a multivalent joke for the reader. One of Roland Barthes's best-known works is "The Death of the Author," creating both a morbid allusion to the death of Theresa (who creates the child and authors the plan to reunite the family) and a reminder to refuse the conflation of Lee himself with the text.

30. Knapp, "The Business of Forgetting," 217.

31. Ibid., 219, 198.

32. Ibid., 201.

33. Wilhite, "Contested Terrain," 638.

34. Sohn applied the critic Catherine Jurca's concept of "sentimental dispossession," the "affective dislocation by which white middleclass [*sic*] suburbanites begin to see themselves as spiritually and culturally impoverished by prosperity," to *Aloft* to conclude that such a position can exist only within white privilege ("White, "White Flight, White Narration," 60).

Chapter 5—"Differing scales, unlikely modulations"

1. Joe Fassler, "Why Novel-Writing Is Like Spelunking: An Interview with Changrae Lee," *Atlantic,* July 11, 2011.

2. While the novel received some mixed reviews, Michiko Kakutani, a longtime champion of Lee's work, called *The Surrendered* "the most ambitious and compelling

novel of his already impressive career" ("Lives Scarred by Horrors of Korean War," *New York Times,* March 8, 2010).

3. Fassler, "Why Novel-Writing Is Like Spelunking."

4. Craig Morgan Teicher, "War Story," *Publisher's Weekly,* January 25, 2010, 88.

5. Uh Soo-woong, "Yes, I Must Be a Freak!," *Korea Focus* (May 2013). Accessed September 26, 2015. www.koreafocus.or.kr.

6. Teicher, "War Story," 88.

7. Ibid.

8. Ibid.

9. For more information about the Korean War, see Max Hastings, *The Korean War* (New York: Simon & Schuster, 1987); David Halberstam, *The Coldest Winter: America and the Korean War* (New York: Hyperion, 2007); and Bruce Cumings, *The Korean War: A History* (New York: Modern Library, 2010).

10. Hsu, "The Ontology of Disability in Chang-rae Lee's *The Surrendered,*" 25.

11. Ibid. Hsu also argued that June Han is "neurodiverse," which serves as a counter to stereotypes of Asians: "Unlike the unspecified state of trauma that is frequently associated with immigrant assimilation in Asian American literature, June's characterization materializes neurodiversity in a way that exceeds the limiting and racist stereotype of the aloof, silent, or inscrutable Asian."

12. Lisa Lowe, *Immigrant Acts: On Asian American Cultural Politics* (Durham, N.C.: Duke University Press, 1996), 16.

13. Michiko Kakutani, "Lives Scarred by Horrors of Korean War," *New York Times,* March 8, 2010. In Kakutani's opinion, Hector "sometimes feels more like a symbol than a human being, and the deaths that pile up around him—including those of his father and several girlfriends—can feel contrived, like the self-conscious manipulations of an author intent on exploring the equation of fate and free will." This interpretation of Hector paralleled later critiques of the central character in *On Such a Full Sea.*

14. Ha Jin's *War Trash* (2004) is one of the few novels focused solely on the Korean War. Told from the perspective of a Chinese POW in an American camp, the novel reads like a gripping memoir.

15. See Yoshihisa Tak Matsusaka, *The Making of Japanese Manchuria, 1904–1932* (Cambridge, Mass.: Harvard University Asia Center, 2001), for the history leading up to the Japanese occupation of Manchuria. See Louise Young, *Japan's Total Empire: Manchuria and the Culture of Wartime Imperialism* (Berkeley: University of California Press, 1998), for the history of Manchukuo until Japanese defeat in 1945.

16. Much like the main character in Marguerite Dumas's 1984 novel *The Lover,* thirteen-year-old Sylvie is infatuated with her older Chinese tutor. Though she clumsily instigates a sexual encounter that gratifies him, she remains a virgin, and they resume her lessons without discussing the incident.

17. In *The Surrendered* two missionaries tell the Binets of the deaths of Lutheran missionaries in the Congo in the late 1920s and compare this ruthless violence to the actions of the Japanese in China: "the Japanese wiped a few villages off the map. Eradicated every last soul" (184). As in *A Gesture Life,* Lee highlights the brutality of imperial Japan in its quest for dominance in the region.

18. Arissa Oh, "From War Waif to Ideal Immigrant: The Cold War Transformation of the Korean Orphan," *Journal of American Ethnic History* 31.4 (Summer 2012): 43–44. In this fascinating article, Oh argued that the adoption of Korean children after

the war led to the acceptance of Asian immigrants more widely, which contributed to the end of the anti-Asian quota system within U.S. immigration law.

19. Arissa Oh, "A New Kind of Missionary Work: Christians, Christian Americanists, and the Adoption of Korean GI Babies, 1955–1961," *Women's Studies Quarterly* 33.3–4 (Fall–Winter 2005): 165.

20. Hsu, "The Ontology of Disability in Chang-rae Lee's *The Surrendered*," 30. Hsu refers here to "crip" theory which is a branch of disability studies that attempts to revalue the word "crippled" to indicate inclusion of disability as a form identity in a manner that parallels the reclamation of "queer" in academic and popular discourse.

21. Oh, "From War Waif to Ideal Immigrant," 48.

22. Hsu, "The Ontology of Disability in Chang-rae Lee's *The Surrendered*," 32–33.

23. In *On Such a Full Sea*, Lee repeats a similar ghostly echo from *The Surrendered* but with a decidedly more pointed twist on those who demand recognition in the form of the smell lofting from the ancient sewers of the lower classes: "after there's a heavy rain and the wind blows from the southwest, you can pick up from our very block the sharp rot stink of human settlement, that undying herald: We are here! We are here! We are here! . . . We know you are there, believe us" (13).

Chapter 6—"A special conviction of imagination"

1. Sarah Anne Johnson, "Chang-rae Lee: The Drama of Consciousness," in *The Very Telling: Conversations with American Writers* (Lebanon, N.H.: University Press of New England, 2006), 110.

2. Michiko Kakutani, "Sacrificing Gated Safety for a Lover and Herself," *New York Times*, January 12, 2014.

3. Though the actual date of the narration is undetermined, Lee reported in one interview that "the time period . . . is about 150 or 200 years from now, not a thousand years from now, not fifty"; see David Naimon, "A Conversation with Chang-rae Lee," *Missouri Review* 37.1 (Spring 2014): 124.

4. Christopher T. Fan, "Future Islands," *New Inquiry Magazine*, May 19, 2014.

5. Naimon, "A Conversation," 124.

6. Maud Newton, "Wave of the Future: Chang-rae Lee," *Barnes and Noble Review*, January 7, 2014. Accessed July 25, 2016. www.barnesandnoble.com/review/.

7. Lee has described abandoning a novel on Chinese factory towns before beginning *On Such a Full Sea*: "I began writing a novel about them and their bosses, but soon dropped the project, as I wondered if I was adding anything fresh to the already abundant and excellent journalism about life in China. A novel, even a social realist one, can't simply be a comprehensive rendering of what is. A novel requires a special angle or approach, whether in structure or language or theme, to justify itself. I didn't quite have that angle"; see Cressida Leyshon, "The Chorus of 'We': An Interview with Chang-rae Lee," *New Yorker*, January 6, 2014.

8. Chang-rae Lee, "Isn't All Immigrant Fiction Essentially Dystopian Fiction?" Accessed July 25, 2016. www.penguinrandomhouse.com.

9. Boris Kachka, "Pigging Out with Writers Gary Shteyngart and Chang-rae Lee," *Vulture*, January 7, 2014.

10. Meredith Turits, "The Rumpus Interview with Chang-rae Lee," *Rumpus*, March 4, 2014.

11. The authors whom Lee cited as influences and favorites in this interview also reflect his desire to be positioned in dialogue with the "greats" of Western literature; the list is predominately male and predominately white. See "Chang-rae Lee: By the Book," *New York Times Sunday Book Review*, January 23, 2014.

12. Lee's efforts to mitigate the novel's reception as dystopian may also serve to undercut the criticism of his novel from those who measured the novel against serious dystopian fiction. Appearing in the *Guardian* on January 30, 2014, Ursula K. Le Guin's review of *On Such a Full Sea* was subtitled "Every Literary Writer Seems to Visit Dystopia Now—But Too Many Treat a Serious Genre Superficially." Le Guin scathingly noted that none of the pragmatic concerns of Lee's imagined future world are explained, to the novel's detriment:

> In a broken, sporadic civilization, where does all this stuff come from? Neglect of such literal, rational questions in imaginative fiction is often excused, even legitimized, as literary licence. Because the author is known as a literary writer, he will probably be granted the licence he takes. But social science fiction is granted no such irresponsibility, and a novel about a future society under intense political control is social science fiction. Like Cormac McCarthy and others, Lee uses essential elements of a serious genre irresponsibly, superficially. As a result, his imagined world carries little weight of reality. The whole system is too self-contradictory to serve as a warning or satire, even if towards the end of the book the narrator begins to suspect its insubstantiality.

13. Naimon, "A Conversation," 122.

14. Leyshon, "The Chorus of 'We.'"

15. Jiayang Fan, "New America and Old China in Dystopian Novels," *Virginia Quarterly Review* 90 (Spring 2014): 227.

16. Andrew Sean Greer, "Diving into the Wreck," *New York Times,* January 2, 2014.

17. Maureen Corrigan, "Chang-rae Lee Stretches for Dystopic Drama, but Doesn't Quite Reach," National Public Radio, January 14, 2014.

18. Naimon, "A Conversation," 131.

19. Chuh, "One Hundred Percent Korean," 108.

20. Lee's class commentary extends to critiquing the disparity in American relationships to food. He skewers the elitism of what he calls the "Back to Soil" movement that stresses natural purity for Charters even as those in the country struggle for basic survival (*On Such a Full Sea,* 100): "Charters are famously nervous, for despite their wealth and security and self-satisfied demeanors, they are obsessed with minimizing hazards of any kind, and are perhaps racked most of all by the finally unknowable dangers of what they ingest. It's the only thing that they have not mastered" (99).

This scene perhaps shows the influence of Don DeLillo's classic *White Noise* (1985), one of Lee's favorite novels: "That's a book about a lot of things: consumerism again, American storytelling through this deadened language of commerce, but it is also filled with these waves of radiation, and airborne toxic events, this ominous atmosphere literally over the landscape, that we are infected by our society in ways that we just can't quite grasp, and if we could grasp it we would be horrified" (Naimon, "A Conversation," 131).

21. Leyshon, "The Chorus of 'We.'"

22. Naimon, "A Conversation," 126.

23. Here, Lee comments on the popularity of Asian blepharoplasty, or double eyelid surgery, among young women. Although attitudes toward this cosmetic surgery are mixed, these abused characters are driven by a desire to erase their identities, so there can be little doubt of Lee's feelings about this procedure. For another literary treatment of this topic, see An Na's young adult novel *The Fold* (Putnam, 2008).

24. Anime and manga too are frequently critiqued for depicting Asian characters as white or Western. Dana Fennell, Ana S. Q. Liberato, Bridge Hayden, and Yuko Fujino, "Consuming Anime," *Television & News Media* 14.5 (2012): 440–56, traced the conflicting attitudes about racial depictions in these forms. This article pointed out that while some critics argued that "white" appearing characters "reinforce theories of anime as not containing Japanese 'cultural odor' but potentially the cultural odor of other groups," still other critics argued that "since anime characters can have wildly colored hair and unrealistic body shapes," these depictions are instead uniquely characteristic of the form, not race (442).

25. Leyshon, "The Chorus of 'We.'"

26. See chapter 1 for a discussion of Lee's decision to keep his name upon going to school.

27. See chapter 1 for a discussion of Lee's mother's painful death from cancer.

28. Lee has noted that these lines from *Julius Caesar* provided some of the defining imagery of the novel: "Even though [Brutus is] speaking metaphorically, just the image of it, this tide, this wave that this little girl would be on. Does the wave come from herself, or does it come from outside? She seems so persistent and irrepressible in a certain way, and I love that idea of the sea rising, and that she was a diver, and I thought, 'That's perfect'" (Newton, "Wave of the Future").

29. In addition to the hardcover edition with the illustration designed by Helen Yentus, another limited-edition hardcover edition was available in what was marketed as the first 3-D printed slipcover for a book.

30. Lee described the danger in creating a heroine like Fan: "All the things that we have now are about revealing private moments of consciousness, and sharing them with each other. A constantly defining and redefining of each other and ourselves by all this stuff. And it's exhausting. And the thought experiment for me artistically was: could I write a story in which the main character had none of that stuff? But you'd still feel something for her, and care about her, if you didn't really know her. And what was that? That seems to me elementally what a hero is. It's not because we know them so well. They're magnetic. It's a different kind of charisma"; see Emma Brockes, "Chang-rae Lee: 'When people asked, I'd say, "I'm writing a very strange book." I thought no one was going to get it,'" *Guardian*, January 19, 2014.

31. Naimon, "A Conversation," 127.

32. Chuh, "One Hundred Percent Korean," 109.

33. Juliana Chang, "Romantic Citizenship," 125.

34. Ibid., 128.

35. Le Guin, however, rejected the success of Fan as a character: "Her superheroism is coloured by a tinge of saintliness ascribed to her by the elusive first-person-plural narrator—the voice of the industrious, modest, patient workers of her home hive. Perhaps she represents their virtues. I could believe in those virtues, but I could not believe in Fan" (Le Guin, "*On Such a Full Sea* by Chang-rae Lee").

36. Brockes in "Chang-rae Lee" wrote, "It was Lee's own daughters who partly

inspired him to write the book; he has a 13- and a 16-year-old, and he wanted to write something they might potentially enjoy, or create a heroine they might identify with." The novel is dedicated to them.

37. In an interview with Maud Newton, Lee expressed confusion over the apathy of the United States toward the nation's extreme economic disparity; see Newton, "Wave of the Future."

38. Naimon, "A Conversation," 132.

BIBLIOGRAPHY

Primary Works

NOVELS

Native Speaker. New York: Riverhead Books, 1995.
A Gesture Life. New York: Riverhead Books, 1999.
Aloft. New York: Riverhead Books, 2004.
The Surrendered. New York: Riverhead Books, 2010.
On Such a Full Sea. New York: Riverhead Books, 2014.

ESSAYS

"The Faintest Echo of Our Language." *New England Review* 15.3 (Summer 1993): 85–92.
"Coming Home Again." *New Yorker,* October 16, 1995.
"Mute in an English-Only World." *New York Times,* April 18, 1996.
"Uncle Chul Gets Rich." *New York Times Magazine,* May 12, 1996.
"Beans." *New Yorker*, December 23, 1996.
"My Suburb: Ridgewood, N.J." *New York Times Magazine,* April 9, 2000.
"The Spicy Pleasures of Phuket." *New York Times Magazine*, May 14, 2000.
"Sea Urchin." *New Yorker,* August 19, 2002.
"Eat, Memory." *New York Times Magazine*, October 10, 2004.
"Passages to Italy: A Wine to Remember." *Food and Wine* (September 2007).
"Understanding Oregon Pinot Noir Country." *Food and Wine* (October 2009).
"Remembering Salinger." *Page-Turner* (blog), *New Yorker*, January 28, 2010. Accessed July 25, 2016. http://www.newyorker.com/books/page-turner.
"Magical Dinners." *New Yorker*, November 22, 2010.
"A Case for Wine on the Web." *Food and Wine*, October 2011.
"Manhattan." *New Yorker*, December 3, 2012.
"Immoveable Feast." *New Yorker,* November 3, 2014.

Secondary Works

Ang, Sze Wei. "The Politics of Victimization and the Model Minority." *New Centennial Review* 11.3 (2012): 119–39.
Arac, Jonathan. "Violence and the Human Voice: Critique and Hope in *Native Speaker.*" *Boundary 2: An International Journal of Literature and Culture* 36.2 (2009): 55–66.
Carroll, Hamilton. "Traumatic Patriarchy: Reading Gendered Nationalisms in Chang-rae Lee's *A Gesture Life.*" *Modern Fiction Studies* 51.3 (2005): 592–616.

Caton, Lou Freitas. "A Korean American Perspective: Tolerating Truth and Knowledge in Chang-rae Lee's *Native Speaker.*" In *Reading American Novels and Multicultural Aesthetics: Romancing the Postmodern Novel,* 121–37. New York: Palgrave Macmillan, 2008.

Chang, Juliana. "Romantic Citizenship: Immigrant-Nation Romance, the Antifetish, and Chang-rae Lee's *Native Speaker.*" In *Inhuman Citizenship: Traumatic Enjoyment and Asian American Literature,* 107–45. Minneapolis: University of Minnesota Press, 2012.

Chang, Yoonmee. "Ethnic Entrepreneurs: Korean American Spies, Shopkeepers, and the 1992 Los Angeles Riots." In *Writing the Ghetto: Class, Authorship, and the Asian American Ethnic Enclave,* 135–75. New Brunswick, N.J.: Rutgers University Press, 2010.

Chen, Tina. "Impersonation and Other Disappearing Acts in *Native Speaker* by Chang-rae Lee." *Modern Fiction Studies* 48.3 (2002): 637–67.

Cheng, Anne Anlin. "Passing, Natural Selection, and Love's Failure: Ethics of Survival from Chang-rae Lee to Jacques Lacan." *American Literary History* 17.3 (2005): 553–74.

Chua, Cheng Lok. "Asian Americans Imagining Burma: Chang-rae Lee's *A Gesture Life* and Wendy Law-Yone's *Irrawaddy Tango.*" In *Bloom's Modern Critical Views: Asian-American Writers,* edited by Harold Bloom, 139–49. New York: Infobase, 2009.

Chuh, Kandice. *Imagine Otherwise: On Asian Americanist Critique.* Durham, N.C.: Duke University Press, 2003.

———. "'One Hundred Percent Korean': On Space and Subjectivity." In *Imagine Otherwise: On Asian Americanist Critique,* 85–111. Durham, N.C.: Duke University Press, 2003.

Corley, Liam. "'Just Another Ethnic Pol': Literary Citizenship in Chang-rae Lee's *Native Speaker.*" *Studies in the Literary Imagination* 37.1 (Spring 2004): 61–81.

Cowart, David. "Korean Connection: Chang-rae Lee and Company." In *Trailing Clouds: Immigrant Fiction in Contemporary America,* 101–25. Ithaca, N.Y.: Cornell University Press, 2006.

Dwyer, June. "Ethnic Home Improvement: Gentrifying the Ghetto, Spicing Up the Suburbs." *Interdisciplinary Studies in Literature and Environment* 14.2 (2007): 165–82.

Engles, Tim. "Visions of Me in the Whitest Raw Light: Assimilation and Doxic Whiteness in Chang-rae Lee's *Native Speaker.*" *Hitting Critical Mass* 4.2 (Summer 1997): 27–48.

Hsu, Stephanie. "The Ontology of Disability in Chang-rae Lee's *The Surrendered.*" *Journal of Literary and Cultural Disability Studies* 7.1 (2013): 19–35.

Huang, Betsey. "Chang-rae Lee and the Counter-Gestures of Life Writing." In *Contesting Genres in Contemporary Asian American Fiction,* 29–45. New York: Palgrave Macmillan, 2010.

———. "Citizen Kwang: Chang-rae Lee's *Native Speaker* and the Politics of Consent." *Journal of Asian American Studies* 9.3 (October 2006): 243–69.

Hurst, Mary Jane. "Balancing Self and Other through Speech and Silence in Chang-rae Lee's *Native Speaker* and Amy Tan's *The Hundred Secret Senses.*" In *Language, Gender, and Community in Late Twentieth-Century Fiction,* 77–102. New York: Palgrave, 2011.

Jerng, Mark C. "Nowhere in Particular: Perceiving Race, Chang-rae Lee's *Aloft*, and the Question of Asian American Fiction." *Modern Fiction Studies* 56.1 (Spring 2010): 183–204.

———. "Recognizing the Transracial Adoptee: Adoption Life Stories and Chang-rae Lee's *A Gesture Life*." *Journal of the Society for the Study of the Multi-Ethnic Literature of the United States* 31.2 (2006): 41–67.

Jiayang, Fan. "New America and Old China in Dystopian Novels." *Virginia Quarterly Review* 90.2 (2014): 227–30.

Jirousek, Lori. "'A New Book of the Land': Ethnography, Espionage, and Immigrants in *Native Speaker*." *Modern Language Studies* 36.1 (2006): 8–23.

Kim, Daniel Y. "Do I, Too, Sing America? Vernacular Representations and Chang-rae Lee's *Native Speaker*." *Journal of Asian American Studies* 6.3 (October 2003): 231–60.

Kim, Jodi. "From Mee-Gook to Gook: The Cold War and Racialized Undocumented Capital in Chang-rae Lee's *Native Speaker*." *Journal of the Society for the Study of the Multi-Ethnic Literature of the United States* 34.1 (2009): 117–37.

Knapp, Kathy. "The Business of Forgetting: Postwar Living Memorials and the Post-Traumatic Suburb in Chang-rae Lee's *Aloft*." *Twentieth Century Literature* 59.2 (2013): 196–231.

Kong, Belinda. "Beyond K's Specter: Chang-rae Lee's *A Gesture Life*, Comfort Women Testimonies, and Asian American Transnational Aesthetics." *Journal of Transnational American Studies* 3.1 (2011).

Lee, Christopher. "Form-Giving and the Remains of Identity in *A Gesture Life*." *Journal of Asian American Studies* 14.1 (February 2011): 95–116.

Lee, James Kyung-Jin. "Where the Talented Tenth Meets the Model Minority: The Price of Privilege in Wideman's *Philadelphia Fire* and Lee's *Native Speaker*." *Novel: A Forum on Fiction* 35.2–3 (2002): 231–57.

Lee, Kun Jong. "Towards Interracial Understanding and Identification: Spike Lee's *Do the Right Thing* and Chang-rae Lee's *Native Speaker*." *Journal of American Studies* 44.4 (2010): 741–57.

Lee, Rachel C. "Reading Contests and Contesting Reading: Chang-rae Lee's *Native Speaker* and Ethnic New York." *Journal of the Society for the Study of the Multi-Ethnic Literature of the United States* 29.3–4 (2004): 341–52.

Lee, So-Hee. "Cultural Citizenship as Subject-Making in *Comfort Woman* and *A Gesture Life*." *Feminist Studies in English Literature* 14.2 (2006): 91–123.

Lee, Young-Oak. "Transcending Ethnicity Diasporicity in *A Gesture Life*." *Journal of Asian American Studies* 12.1 (February 2009): 65–81.

Ludwig, Sämi. "Ethnicity as Cognitive Identity: Private and Public Negotiations in Chang-rae Lee's *Native Speaker*." *Journal of Asian American Studies* 10.3 (October 2007): 221–42.

Miller, Matthew. "Chang-rae Lee's *A Gesture Life:* The Recuperation of Identity." *Ethnic Studies Review: The Journal of the National Association for Ethnic Studies* 32.2 (2009): 1–24.

Moraru, Christian. "The Other, the Namesake: Cosmopolitan Onomastics in Change-rae Lee's *A Gesture Life*." *Names: A Journal of Onomastics* 55.1 (2007): 17–35.

———. "Speakers and Sleepers: Chang-rae Lee's *Native Speaker*, Whitman, and the Performance of Americanness." *College Literature* 36.3 (2009): 66–91.

Motuz, Alexis. "Before Speech: An Interrogation of Trauma in Chang-rae Lee's *A Gesture Life*." *Canadian Review of American Studies/Revue Canadienne D'etudes Americaines* 43.3 (2013): 411–32.

Narkunas, J. Paul. "Surfing the Long Waves of Global Capital with Chang-rae Lee's *Native Speaker:* Ethnic Branding and the Humanization of Capital." *Modern Fiction Studies* 54.2 (2008): 327–52.

Parikh, Crystal. "Ethnic America Undercover: The Intellectual and Minority Discourse." *Contemporary Literature* 43.2 (2002): 249–84.

Park, You-me, and Gayle Wald. "Native Daughters in the Promised Land: Gender, Race, and the Question of Separate Spheres." *American Literature: A Journal of Literary History, Criticism, and Bibliography* 70.3 (1998): 607–33.

Rhee, Michelle Young-Mee. "'Greater Lore': Metafiction in Chang-rae Lee's *Native Speaker*." *Journal of the Society for the Study of the Multi-Ethnic Literature of the United States* 36.1 (2011): 157–76.

Rhee, Suk Koo. "Consumable Bodies and Ethnic (Hi)Stories: Strategies and Risks of Representation in *A Gesture Life*." *Discourse: Journal for Theoretical Studies in Media and Culture* 34.1 (2012): 93–112.

Rody, Caroline. "'With Darkness Yet': Chang-rae Lee's *Native Speaker,* Blackness, and the Interethnic Imagination." In *The Interethnic Imagination: Roots and Passages in Contemporary Asian American Fiction,* 66–88. New York: Oxford University Press, 2009.

Sedlmeier, Florian. "Rereading Literary Form: Paratexts, Transpositions, and Postethnic Literature around 2000." *Journal of Literary Theory* 6.1 (2012): 213–34.

Sohn, Stephen Hong. "White Flight, White Narration: Suburban Deviancies in Chang-rae Lee's *Aloft*." In *Racial Asymmetries: Asian American Fictional Worlds,* 25–62. New York: New York University Press, 2014.

Song, Min Hyoung. "A Diasporic Future? *Native Speaker* and Historical Trauma." *Literature Interpretation Theory* 12.1 (2001): 79–98.

Tsou, Elda E. "'This Doesn't Mean What You'll Think': *Native Speaker,* Allegory, Race." *Publications of the Modern Language Association of America* 128.3 (2013): 575–89.

Varvogli, Aliki. "Chang-rae Lee, *A Gesture Life;* Ethan Canin, *Carry Me across the Water*." In *Travel and Dislocation in Contemporary American Fiction,* 96–116. New York: Routledge, 2012.

Wilhite, Keith. "Contested Terrain: The Suburbs as Region." *American Literature* 84.3 (September 2012): 617–44.

Wills, Jenny Heijun. "Claiming America by Claiming Others: Asian-American Adoptive Parenthood in *A Gesture Life* and *Digging to America*." *Americana: The Journal of American Popular Culture (1900–Present)* 10.1 (2011).Accessed July 25, 2016. www.americanpopularculture.com/journal/.

Wu, Yung-Hsing. "Native Sons and Native Speakers: On the Eth(N)Ics of Comparison." *Publications of the Modern Language Association of America* 121.5 (2006): 1460–74.

Xiang, Sunny. "The Korean Voice of American Empire: The Democratic Spokesman and the Model Minority Narrator." *Journal of Asian American Studies* 17.3 (October 2014): 273–304.

INDEX